W9-BZG-014

The Bride

The Bride

One Woman's Walk
Through Judaism & Catholicism:
The Sabbath, Marriage, Mass,
and the World to Come

The Miriam Press
4120 W. Pine Blvd.
Saint Louis, MO 63108

Cover image credit:
© "Bright Star of David" by Dan Paulos,
Courtesy of Trinity Stores, http://trinitystores.com,
800-669-4482

www.hebrewcatholic.net
tmp@hebrewcatholic.org

ISBN: 978-0-939409-09-9
Library of Congress Control Number: 2017955975

TABLE OF CONTENTS

Preface

Explorers need a map. The journey of Channah Bardan in the following pages is itself a map of exploration "back to the future," to borrow an old movie title. The map unfolds and is recorded along with the journey itself. Although this exploration has taken place on the ground in real geographical locations, its origin is in eternity. The energy, love, and will to discover the path forward have fueled this voyage in a vessel navigated by the light of the Master's timeless coordinates.

Departing from St. Louis, Missouri in 1804 for an exploration of the Missouri River which was commissioned by President Thomas Jefferson, explorers Lewis and Clark prepared as well as possible in advance for the unknown. Lewis undertook special studies for the journey, and a special keelboat was constructed which they thought would be best in navigating the river. Part of their mission was to see if there was fertile ground along the unexplored westward river where more settlers could later follow and develop the land. One task that Lewis and Clark had to undertake which was critical to their mission was to record and commit their journey to the written page. They did so. Reminiscent of the expedition of Lewis and Clark, Bardan blazes herein a modern-day spiritual trail not previously traveled for about the last 1,700 years. In her own written record, she has indeed discovered rich and fertile ground ahead.

If in these pages the reader searches prematurely for precise and official Catholic and/or Jewish theological parameters, then perhaps this journey will not yet command your attention. This same reader might even seriously question the validity of practicing a devout Catholic life while embracing within Christ all that is true and beautiful in Judaism.

However, if the reader is searching for the forward journey itself, willing to be electrified herein by a passionate love for God as lived out with zeal in the amazing embrace of both Orthodox Jewish practices and fervent Catholicism, then you can rejoice in these pages. You are already engaged in the journey forward. You might even exult that one woman has traveled into uncharted territory led by the all-consuming lifetime experience of her identity as God's fully Jewish and then fully Catholic daughter. It is a work in progress.

Bardan was teethed on the riches and beauty and orderliness of Orthodox Judaism. When God led her yet deeper into the riches and fullness of Catholicism, she could only channel the joy and motivation of her overflowing life by feasting daily in the deep reality of both traditions. In this work of joy, she has poured out upon her many friends and readers the love of God revealed with vigor in her written record. There is a demand for a book such as this, at this very time in salvation history.

As we witness daily the breakdown of what was once Judeo-Christian culture, the spiritual warfare against natural law, and so often now the rejection of even the very concept of eternal salvation by a Messiah, we also witness God's victory ahead of time by faith! He is victorious on behalf of His beloved Jewish people, and He is victorious on behalf of His beloved nations. To those who receive Him, both Jewish and non-Jewish peoples, Christ unifies all in Himself, brings all into reconciliation with God, and all is at rest in His Kingdom.

Our Blessed Mother Mary exemplifies in Catholicism all that has been passed down through holy Jewish tradition as true and beautiful and pure for women. Honoring the call "to Jesus through Mary," Bardan has given us a generous glimpse into her own role as a modern Hebrew Catholic woman who is fulfilling her role as guardian of her own home in holiness. She invokes every opportunity for her and her family to experience the spiritual intimacy of "wedded" love that God offers to all of us. She has made room for it.

Enthralling is this journey into a seamless unity of the *Old* and *New* treasures through Christ, and rare is the person who has the lived experience plus the energy and the will to attempt it. We depend on the faithful slow workings of the Holy Spirit in the Church to expand our vision on the road ahead. In our day, Orthodox Jews are bringing life-giving spiritual treasures as the pathway opens in God's time, and *The Bride* is one such treasure, infused as it is by the spirit of truth, beauty, and holiness in Christ. Nuptial intimacy with God and His love can only be found at very close range. This book is a tale of passion for God and others at close range, love's range.

Is *The Bride* "correct" theologically in light of the Word Incarnate, Jesus Christ, and the divinely revealed grandeur of true Catholicism? What is Catholicism, if not the passionate outpouring of God's love first to His Chosen People and then to all His other people grafted into the Chosen people through Christ and adopted as true sons and daughters in God's family? What is "incorrect" about practicing revered elements of your own ancient Jewish tradition within your home, all in full accord with true Catholic doctrine, and discovering that it works beautifully to magnify and deepen your union with God?

Who could have attempted this exhilarating journey except one who was schooled from birth in the treasures of Orthodox Judaism in a loving family – who was then catapulted by grace into the Kingdom of the Bridegroom,

Jesus Christ, the Second Person of the Holy Trinity, the King of the Jews – and who has already engaged on a daily basis this courageous embrace of two traditions woven into one within her own loving family, husband and children?

One might say that this book richly presents in microcosm everything that the Association of Hebrew Catholics (AHC) works to promote in helping to fulfill God's will for the Jewish people within His Church.

The Bride weds everything that points to the Messiah in certain revered traditions of Orthodox Judaism to the incarnate Son of God in the Eucharistic sacrifice of the Mass. What more evangelical witness could Jewish people in the Church manifest than to render glory to God by exulting in and practicing the treasures of both the *Old* and the *New*? (Matthew 13:52)

This is not to say that every Hebrew Catholic will want to embrace this approach to spirituality. Not by any means. There is room for all people in God's net of love – from former atheists to agnostic Jews, from secular to Reform Jews, and from all the varied backgrounds of Jewish people now in the Church or yet to come, beyond ability to mention. But where better to start than with the laser beam holiness and beauty of Orthodox Judaism, culminating in the fullness and grace of authentic Catholicism, where the King of Creation is truly present at the heart of a Jewish family?

> *"For the word of God is living and active, sharper than any two-edged sword, piercing to the division of soul and spirit, of joints and marrow, and discerning the thoughts and intentions of the heart." (Heb. 4:12)*

Some Hebrew Catholics are called to marriage, while others may be called to enter Monasteries or religious communities where the rules of life and devotions are according to the specific charism of the founder. Other Jews may be called to start a new religious community where the wedding of *Old* and *New* can be lived out legitimately and fully, as explored here in *The Bride*.

> *"O Lord my God, you are very great! You are clothed with honor and majesty, who cover yourself with light as with a garment, who have stretched out the heavens like a tent..."* *(Ps 104:1-2)*

God's love is ever creative and expansive, like Himself, and He passionately (if slowly over time) makes room for new forms of authentic worship.

We are not at the end of anything, but always at a new beginning in Our Lord's infinitely fascinating Kingdom. We wait for more souls to respond to God's interior trumpet call until a critical mass is reached and the Church is ready for its promised "life from the dead." (Romans 11:15) When the Jewish people catch fire with their Messiah Jesus Christ in true Catholicism, we will see changes. With the hundreds of thousands of Jews who have already come to believe in Jesus Christ since WWII, we may already be witnessing a phase of that "life from the dead."

Anyone who desires to expand on or improve an approach to authentic Hebrew Catholic spirituality, where Jesus Christ is the Alpha and Omega of the law and the prophets, has an open road to take up the challenge. New works of scholarly, and *lived*, Catholic and Jewish exploration on this subject are needed. This is God's work, and His invitation stands open to those who hear His call to jump in the water and walk toward Him.

We give thanks to God for this faith-filled work of Channah Bardan. She has blazed a clear trail straight through a dense forest of interfaith dialogue, theological debate, and controversy concerning the possibility or impossibility of just such a journey as this. She has already crossed through a spiritual Red Sea.

Praised be Jesus Christ, now and forever!

Kathleen M. Moss
Association of Hebrew Catholics

Introduction – The Walk

I was born and raised as an Orthodox Jew in a small Southern town of about 20,000 in the middle of the Bible belt. Fifty years ago, our town was not unique in its make-up of residents of mostly English and Scottish descent. Our economy thrived from the cotton, textile, and tobacco industries. It was a town that prided itself in having more members of the Daughters of the American Revolution and Daughters of the Confederacy, and more churches per capita than other towns of its size. My family, in fact the entire Jewish community, really stood out in what was at that time a very homogeneous society.

Most Jewish communities down South were so small that they could barely support one synagogue. Ours was unusual: With only 50-60 Jewish families, most Jews typically grouped together to form a single congregation – usually Conservative, which is middle-of-the-road – or Reformed, the more liberal of the three branches of Judaism. We were unique in that we had two separate congregations, each with its own house of worship and its own rabbi. The congregation to which my family belonged was Orthodox (very observant). The other was extremely Reformed. Neither synagogue ever had more than 30 families.

Religiously, there was a polar tension between the two sects. In our family, as in other Orthodox households, extreme diligence was required to keep a kosher home in a town where most people had never heard of the laws of *kashrut*, כשרות, (following the dietary laws set forth in Leviticus and by the rabbinic authorities of the Second Temple era in the early years A.D.). No pork or shellfish could be eaten: They were "unclean." Meat products could not be mixed with dairy products at the same meal, and the meat had to be specially prepared. My mother, with the other Orthodox women, would order specialty kosher and ethnically Jewish food from New York, which would arrive each Thursday afternoon at the Greyhound bus station, packed in dry ice. Hopefully, it would have survived the nine-hour bus trip. At the opposite end of the spectrum was our neighbor, J.C.B., a Reform Jew, who would often invite us, with extreme Southern hospitality, to her home for "*Shabbos*[1] ham." Bless her heart!!! Although separate in religious devotion, our community was united socially by B'nai B'rith, the men's fellowship and service organization, Hadassah for women, and Young Judaea for the youth. Our family whole-heartedly and actively supported all three.

My parents were faithful to observe every Sabbath from sundown Friday evening to sundown Saturday evening. It was a glorious time amidst the hustle and bustle of the week. We kept all the Jewish holidays, our family traditions linking us to an ancient past. My parents often took us on trips to visit family in Baltimore or New York for holidays, weddings, Bar Mitzvahs, and vacations, keeping strong ties with close relatives. Each summer, my sister and I attended a camp for Jewish girls in Maryland, and wherever we traveled, we always attended synagogue services. It was a way of connectedness for us in a world that was sometimes not welcoming of our faith.

In a town where zoning laws were common (certain housing developments were closed to Blacks, Jews, and those few others of ethnic diversity), and some club memberships were restricted, the public school system was open to all. It was never easy growing up Jewish in a mostly Christian neighborhood, or attending schools where I was the only Jewish child in the class, and some-

---

1 *Shabbos* is the Yiddish word for the Sabbath.

times in the entire school. Holidays especially differentiated me from the others, as I would be the one to bring a menorah into class at Christmas and recount the Hanukkah story. At Passover, I was the kid with the matzah crackers when everyone else was sharing their goodies from adorably cute Easter baskets.

As a young child, at Christmas I was exposed to the living nativities put on by the local Main Street churches. Each night for a week before Christmas, each church would reenact the Bethlehem scene complete with farm animals and costumed actors. There would be choirs singing carols and hymns. It was such a festive atmosphere, as families would walk the mile from church to church in the brisk night air. My parents allowed me to go as a learning and cultural experience. I knew right away there was something special about that little baby doll in the manger – special, yet forbidden. I soon found out how forbidden the next day when I wrapped myself in blue towels and my baby doll in blankets and knelt before Him in adoration at the hearth. When my mother came into the living room and saw what I was doing, she exploded. I was not allowed to ever do that again. Living nativities were then replaced with driving through the neighborhoods to see the lights and decorations of the *Goyim.*[2] Decorating our house for Christmas, no matter how tasteful or non-denominational, was another thing we, as Jews, did not do.

Several years later, my Girl Scout troop would visit the Lutheran church to see the Chrismon Tree, a Christmas tree rich with religious symbolism. I remember being struck by the beauty and piety of the handmade decorations of white and gold, each having a Biblical reference. Sometime in grade school, some of the Christian

---

2 *Goyim* is Hebrew for *the nations* and Yiddish for *Gentiles.*

kids witnessed to me. I didn't come away with much, but I remember saying my Hebrew prayers at bedtime with a mental "in Jesus' name" tacked on to the end as a spiritual insurance policy that those prayers would be heard and covered. As time passed and I would try to explain my Jewish faith to the evangelical Baptists and Assemblies of G-d,[3] it became harder to reconcile the fulfillment of all those Old Testament Messianic prophecies I had heard and read about with the person of Jesus.

Even with all the years of *Shabbat* School and Hebrew lessons, I was hungering for more. I wanted to have the opportunity to go up to the altar and say the blessings over the *Torah* scroll. I wanted to read from the *Torah* just as the men did in synagogue.[4] In the Orthodox Jewish community, it is mandated that the men and the women sit separately. The women of our *"shul"* had a lovely balcony overlooking the synagogue floor, which is where I would sit with my mother and the rest of the women. There was absolutely no way I would be able to join in with the men during the liturgy. It was unheard of – a *"shanda"* – or scandalous! So at my pleading, my parents made the sacrifice to transition from the Orthodox to the Reform synagogue when I was 12. I would be the first girl, even there, to be allowed to study to become a *Bat Mitzvah*. This is a momentous rite of passage, which, up until the Feminist Movement of the 1970's, was traditionally taken only by Jewish boys at the age of 13. After years of study in Hebrew, Scripture, and Jewish tradition, the adolescent becomes a *Bar/Bat Mitzvah* (a Son or Daughter of the Commandments), in a synagogue service, leading the liturgy (mostly in Hebrew), reading from the *Torah* scroll in Hebrew for the first time, and delivering a personal commentary on that reading.

3 Out of respect, and adhering to Jewish custom that the name of the Holy One not be uttered or written in full form, I will be using the abbreviated "G-d" from here on.
4 The *Torah* is the Hebrew word for the first five books of Moses in the Scriptures.

I received my first English translation of the Scriptures as a gift from the rabbi for my *Bat Mitzvah*. As I began reading, I began to have even more questions. In the very first chapter of Genesis, verse 26, I read, *"Let **us** make man in **our** image."* And reading a little further about the tower of Babel in Genesis 11: *"And the Lord said... 'Come, let **us** go down, and confound their language...'"* Totally confused about this plurality, I began to voice these concerns. My parents, wiser relatives, and rabbis all had different explanations for the words of these troubling passages. Some stated it was because G-d speaks in the "Royal We" as in Shakespearean English; one person told me that this must be a typo; and a rabbi told me it was because G-d entered into a covenant with the earth/ground itself to form Adam, thus the "us." All I could see was, at best, a multiplural noun for the word G-d, like the English words *team* or *family*. Not an indivisible One. This was also reinforced by the daily recitation of the *Shema* prayer from Deuteronomy, which proclaims, *"Hear, O Israel! The Lord, our G-d, the Lord, is One."* In this case the word *one* is *echad*, אחד, one existing in unity, a multiplural noun. None of the explanations by others satisfied me, and my growing litany of questions, not only about Scripture, but about tradition as well, all seemed to point to Avinu, G-d the Father, *Jesus*, ישוע, *Yeshua* as the promised Hebrew Messiah, and the *Ruach Ha Kodesh, the Holy Spirit.*

Although I maintained a strong Jewish identity throughout high school, as a hopelessly romantic and somewhat dramatic teenage girl, I was drawn to the Catholic Church as portrayed by Hollywood and literature. Jennifer Jones in *The Song of Bernadette* drew me into the holiness of a simple peasant girl transformed into a handmaid of the Lord. Debbie Reynolds' *Singing Nun* left me with the impression of a Holy Sister in a pure white habit with the joy of the Lord, self-sacrificing and walking in love toward all.

Ingrid Bergman's *Joan of Arc* presented a powerful model of stalwart zeal for G-d and country. In my reading, a holy innocent martyr's death was a noble and dramatic ideal. As Flannery O'Connor wrote from The Girl's perspective in her short story, *A Temple of the Holy Ghost,*

> *"She would have to be a saint... she could stand to be shot but not to be burned in oil. She didn't know if she could stand to be torn to pieces by lions or not. She began to prepare her martyrdom seeing herself in a pair of tights in a great arena lit by the early Christians hanging in cages of fire, making a gold, dusty light that fell on her and the lions. The first lion fell at her feet, converted. A whole series of lions did the same. And finally the Romans were obliged to burn her, but to their astonishment, she would not burn down, and finding her so hard to kill, they finally cut off her head very quickly with a sword, and she immediately went to heaven."*

Quite strong stuff to feed the dreams of youth!

During my college years, I continued my inner struggle with religion. After becoming president of the small campus Hillel Jewish Student Organization (even at the large Southern university I attended, there were only about 15 or 20 practicing Jewish students), I would sometimes visit the Newman Club for Catholic university students, asking a reluctant priest about conversion. My two roommates and most of my friends were Catholics. My best friend in school, and later-to-be husband, was brought up in a Catholic home (so... I thought he was Jewish at first!), although when I met him, he was Atheist/Agnostic. John and I often had heady conversations late into the night on topics of history, philosophy, religion, and man's existence.

A few years later after we had both graduated, found jobs, and finally decided to marry, neither family was supportive. We planned a small, non-denominational ceremony in a chapel in California where we were living. My mother traveled across the country to stop the wedding – she tried for that whole week prior, right up until the moment I walked down the aisle!!! – while my father and sister remained at home and held an actual Jewish funeral for me. They observed the seven days of mourning, *shiva*, and recited the *Kaddish* prayers for the dead over me. Now, that's drama! John's entire family had a last-minute change of heart and decided to attend the nuptials.

At the time of our marriage, neither John nor I was affiliated with any religion. We were on the fast track to career, money, and having fun in sunny Southern California. Three months after our wedding, a cyst which had been growing in one of my ovaries ruptured. Lying on the hospital gurney in the hallway of the operating theater, the doctor came over to explain that because one ovary must be removed, and because of endometriosis and blocked fallopian tubes, there was more than a distinct probability that I would be unable to have children. One of the many reasons I had married John was that we both wanted to have a family, and I knew he would be an exceptional father. Having children was a strong desire of both our hearts. As I was wheeled into the surgical suite, I prayed to G-d that if He was real, and if Jesus was the true Messiah – if I could only become pregnant in three to five years – that I would dedicate my life and the child's life to Jesus, fully and openly. Five months later, I found out I was expecting and knew I had a promise to fulfill.

Shortly after my first daughter was born 24 years ago, I entered the Catholic Church. After a year of intense study, I was initiated into the Sacraments during the Easter Vigil. My wonderfully supportive but still non-practicing husband would fully return to the Church four years later, and our marriage would be blessed by the Catholic Church.

My hunger for G-d (which I now fully understand as a fulfillment of all the Messianic prophecies and foreshadowings of the Old Testament) has never stopped. There is so much to study and understand: the sacred Scriptures – the Old Testament and the New Testament in the light of the Old; the glorious history of the Church; the lives and writings of the Saints; divine liturgy and prayer. This ongoing process has further illuminated the Jewish part of my faith, as I now have answers for many of my childhood "whys." Even as a Catholic, I continue to celebrate all of the Jewish holidays in my home and have held onto my Jewish roots. I am as comfortable praying out of a Hebrew *Siddur* as I am from Catholic prayer books. They complement each other, and one enhances the other. Now, as a Jewish Catholic, I feel an even greater intensity about my Jewishness than I did when I was younger.

It has only been recently that I have discovered the full importance of this knowledge, and for me, observance of these roots. I hope with this book to answer some of the many questions I had by showing the symbolism and meaning behind each of the elements of observing the Jewish Sabbath, *Shabbat.* The commandments of the Old Testament to set apart this day along with its developing liturgies are all of Divine origin and all point to *Jesus the Messiah,* ישוע המשיח, *Yeshua HaMashiach* in Hebrew. An understanding of these Jewish roots illuminates many of the parables and teachings of Jesus, who lived a *Torah-observant Jewish life* in the midst of a Torah-observant people. Not only is the *Shabbat* fully realized in the Sacraments of the Catholic Church, but it is a foretaste and dress rehearsal of the *HaOlam Haba,* העולם הבא, *the*

World to Come – our eternity in heaven.[5] In particular, the remembering and keeping of the Sabbath, and the Jewish imagery of the *Sabbath* Bride, lead us straight through the doors of heaven where the true Bridegroom awaits, and to the heavenly banquet table which is the marriage supper of Christ, the Lamb, and his Bride, the community of believers in Him.

---

5 I will be using Hebrew terms for greater authenticity, giving the full English translation.

Chapter 1
Remember and Observe:
Preparing the Way

My Sabbath is a sign between Me and you throughout your generations, that ye may know that I am the Lord who will sanctify you. Ye shall keep the Sabbath therefore, for it is holy unto you.... The children of Israel shall keep the Sabbath, to observe the Sabbath throughout their generations, for a perpetual covenant. It is a sign between Me and the children of Israel for ever; for in six days the Lord made heaven and earth, and on the seventh day He ceased from work and rested.   *Exodus 31:13-17*

Despite the richness of the Catholic Church with its liturgical feasts, rituals, saints, and history, I found I often missed the idea of celebrating the Sabbath in the Jewish tradition. Was I waxing nostalgic, or could it perhaps be something more? In my hectic life of being a home schooling mother of five, with plenty of other extracurricular activities, I never had time for one complete day of rest, let alone an additional Friday/Saturday cessation of work. We never missed Mass on Sunday, but the rest of my weekend was a time to cram all I couldn't get done during the week into this small box of time. Any "extra" time was a rarity, and for me, an opportunity to start or complete another project.

G-d created us in both space and time. Time is at the core of our very being. Scripture says (Genesis 2:2) that on the seventh day, G-d *finished* His work. In Hebrew, and according to the Jewish sages, this word *finished* is an active verb which implies that something did happen. According to ancient tradition, this was when G-d separated the Sabbath to be a time of rest and serenity, *menu-cha*, מנוחה. The Hebrew word forms an active wholeness of peace and harmony in a state of joy. So G-d **actively** ceased His work of creation in order to model the special day joyously presented to us as the gift of the Sabbath. Pope John Paul II in his encyclical *Dies Domini* confirms this by writing,

> *"It speaks, as it were, of G-d's lingering before the 'very good' work (Gen. 1:31) which His hand has wrought, in order to cast upon it a gaze full of joyous delight. This is a contemplative gaze which does not look to new accomplishments but enjoys the beauty of what has already been achieved... It is a gaze which already discloses something of the nuptial shape of the relationship which G-d wants to establish with the creature made in His own image, by calling that creature to enter a pact of love. This is what G-d will gradually accomplish, in offering salvation to all humanity through the saving covenant made with Israel and fulfilled in Christ. It will be the Word Incarnate, through the eschatological gift of the Holy Spirit and the configuration of the Church as His Body and Bride, Who will extend to all humanity the offer of mercy and the call of the Father's love."[1]*

In the chapters to come, I will show how the Sabbath not only is a day of rest, but a type of mystical, holy and joyous marital celebration.

I was always intrigued by the fact that all the days of the week are **ordinary** both figuratively and literally. All the days of the week in Scripture are numbered – the first day, the second day – except for the seventh day, upon which G-d graciously bestows the name *Shabbat* or Sabbath. This designates a day that is extraordinary in G-d's plan. It stands alone among the other days, and it is the most important of all the days of the Jewish week. Where

---

1 Apostolic Letter *Dies Domini* of the Holy Father John Paul II; Section 11; 31 May, 1998.

the other days form the body, *Shabbat* is the soul of the week.

For the Jewish people, and also for the Christian, the Sabbath is a gift. It encompasses a deeper meaning than just the prohibition to do work. In Orthodox and Conservative Judaism, it is forbidden for a person to engage in any activity that alters his environment – in other words, creative work. The point is not the ease or difficulty by which the activity is performed, but the false assumption that comes when we believe we are the true masters of our own destiny. The Sabbath rest reminds us that we are completely dependent upon G-d for everything.

> *"The rest decreed in order to honor the day dedicated to G-d is not at all a burden imposed upon man, but rather an aid to help him to recognize his life-giving and liberating dependence upon the Creator... and to receive his grace,"*

states Pope John Paul II in *Dies Domini.*

> *"In honoring G-d's rest, man fully discovers himself, and thus the Lord's Day bears the profound imprint of His blessing."[2]*

Contemporary theologian and co-chair of the Jewish-Catholic Studies Department at Seton Hall University, Rabbi Asher Finkel states,

> *"Biblical time represents kairos, the opportunity for humankind to enjoy decisive events, while holding the promise of things to come." [3]*

To teach truth through means of visible, tangible objects is an instinct of our human nature. G-d uses this instinct to foretell New Covenant truths (and beyond) to an Old Covenant people. According to the Rabbis of old,

---

2 Ibid.; Section 61.
3 "A Fresh Approach to Jewish Christian Studies," Rabbi Asher Finkel, Service Internationale de Documentation Judeo-Chretienne. Vol. XXVIII, No.2, 1995, page7.

the Spirit of G-d, the *Ruach HaKodesh*, רוח הקודש, writes a religious truth in every object and movement of the *Shabbat* liturgy. Pope John Paul II explains in *Fides et Ratio*, "G-d comes to us in the things we know best and can verify most easily, the things of our everyday life." Each part of the celebration of the Jewish Sabbath is important in teaching a greater spiritual truth.

The theme of *Shabbat* is present in Scripture in a continuous line from the opening of Genesis in the Old Testament through the last book of the *New Testament, Brit Chadasha*, ברת חדשה, the Revelation to St. John. G-d created the entire world, according to the Genesis account, and He, Himself, set apart Day Seven to rest. So important was this day to G-d, a day given as a gift to humanity, rooted so deeply in His divine plan, that in the very center of the Ten Commandments (Exodus 20:8-9), the text reads:

> *"**Remember** the Sabbath day to **keep** it holy. Six days shalt thou labor, and do all thy work. But the seventh day is the Sabbath of the Lord thy G-d: In it thou shalt not do any work, thou nor thy son or daughter, nor thy servant, thy cattle, nor thy stranger that is within thy gates."*

This command to remember the Sabbath is different from, but just as important as, the command to observe the Sabbath.

The Jewish Sabbath begins just before the sun sets on Friday evening and continues until the third star is visible in the night sky on Saturday night. Just as in Catholicism, the Lord's Day begins at the sunset vigil Mass. This comes from the Genesis account of creation, Chapter 1, verse 5, "And there was evening and there was morning", indicating that the day follows the night. When I was growing up, our home, which was typical of Jewish homes throughout the world, had a certain ordered rhythm to the week. As in Exodus 20, Monday through Friday was, in some way, spent remembering the past *Shabbos* and anticipating the *Shabbos* to come. To remember, *zachor*, זכור, entailed waiting and preparing for the next *Shabbos* in order to *shomair*, שומר, to observe it properly. Remembering meant cleaning the house so that everything was beautiful, shining and sparkling. Special foods, not eaten during the week, were planned and prepared. Everything was put in order and made ready and beautiful by each Friday afternoon in anticipation of the 25-hour period to come. Preparation for Friday night and Saturday's divine drama started in earnest on Thursday and continued until Friday evening.

G-d made man with a spirit, soul, and physical bodies. We are sensual beings who understand our world and the Lord Himself by using that wonderful gift of our senses which G-d has given us. In the Jewish realm, the Sabbath is a total sensory experience, full of light and color, taste and texture, sights and smells, music and dance. We cleanse our bodies and dress in our good clothes. The table is set with the best china, silver, and crystal for each Friday evening meal. Fresh flowers are placed on the table and throughout the house. The smells of food cooking all day Friday make the home a warm, inviting place. The two special *challah* breads are baked, and many courses are prepared which will last until Saturday evening. It is a team effort by the whole family (but mostly the mother) and takes a lot of prep work – up to the very last minute on Friday at sunset when all work ceases abruptly. There's **always** the last minute dash of "We're not going to make it!" because once the sun is down, Sabbath **observance** – keeping the Sabbath – starts; no more work can be done. It's all over. Nothing more can be added. All our weekday work is complete. And after all the anticipation, the hour is upon us, and we can rejoice in this delicious time. It is an oasis of love and peace in the desert of the world's hubbub and distraction.

On *Shabbat,* all is in harmony. During the week we deal with work life, school, family issues, bill-paying, appointments to keep. But during the keeping of the Sabbath, all is at peace as we rest in the joy of the home with family, and at synagogue with community. Despite familial quarrels and tensions, *Shabbos* is a time to forgive, or at least to put aside all animosity and bitterness. It is a time of peace – of healing for mind, body, and spirit. It is a time of wholeness: a time to put aside any stressful situation or any unresolved issues with another person.

Missing that old part of my life, and from a deep-seated conviction I would feel during the hectic weekend madness – that I was not just cheating myself and my family, but G-d – I decided to carve out a sacred space and begin to observe the Jewish Sabbath again. The more I studied the Scriptures and began to re-create the traditional observance, the more I understood the importance of the Sabbath. It is not only a day of rest and remembrance of G-d, but a foreshadowing of the *Brit Chadasha,* ברית חדשה, *the New Covenant.* Everything we do in Judaism points unmistakably and directly to the Messiah, *Yeshua,* ישוע *Jesus*; to the Church and our relationship to Jesus; to the Sacramentality of the Church; and to our lives together in the *Ha-Olam Haba,* העולם הבה, *the world to come.*

Now I am enjoying the fullness and richness of both Sabbaths. The ordering of my weekdays ensures everything is finished for the weekend. Somehow, all is getting done. The pace of life is a little less frenetic, and the things of true importance are coming into proper perspective. Time itself seems to have stretched, and this is my first miracle. The observance, rest, and joy of Friday night and

Saturday *Shabbat* prepare me for and heighten my anticipation of the Sunday Mass and family time. I have found
a Messianic Jewish synagogue to attend on Saturday. It is
a congregation of Jewish believers in *Yeshua* as the promised Messiah. The traditional *Shabbat* morning liturgy is
celebrated in Hebrew and English with the same prayers
I remember as a child. The Torah is read in Hebrew as
well as the *Brit Chadasha,* the New Testament. After services is lunch, a Bible study, Hebrew School for the young
ones, and much singing and dancing.

I have now come to a fuller appreciation of all that is
done. I have a new appreciation for the Hebrew liturgy
and order of the service, for these are the same prayers
the Holy Family[4] would have recited every *Shabbat.* This
is exactly what Jesus would have prayed, said, and done...
and much of it was about Him! There is an added dimen-
sion to the holiness of this day. The liturgy of the Jewish service so closely parallels the liturgy of the Catholic
Mass that I feel equally at home in both places. Because
both are rooted and grounded Scripturally, both share
many of the same prayers (the *Kadosh, Kadosh, Kadosh),*
קָדוֹשׁ, קָדוֹשׁ, קָדוֹשׁ, is the same *Holy, Holy, Holy*; the *Avinu,*
אָבִ׳נוּ, uses the same rubrics as the *Our Father*; likewise,
the chanting of the Psalms and Scripture Readings; and
the rabbi's *drash* comes in the same place as the priest's
homily. There is the blessing of the bread and the wine,
which is the root of the Blessed Eucharist, and the final
benediction is often the same as I hear the priest proclaim
at Church. The Jewish Sabbath **should**, in fact, point to
the Mass, which is the high point of our earthly worship.
Both lead to a higher heavenly reality and should serve
to prepare our way to the ultimate celebration in heav-
en, the marriage feast between the Bridegroom and His

---

4 The Holy Family is Jesus, Mary, and Joseph, according to Catholic teaching.

Bride. Pope John Paul II stated, "The Mass we celebrate on earth is a mysterious preparation in the heavenly liturgy." This realization is my second miracle.

Exodus 31:12-17 states,

> *"Then the Lord said to Moses, 'Say to the Israelites, You must observe my Sabbaths. This will be a sign between Me and you for all generations to come, so that you may know that I am the Lord who makes you holy. Observe the Sabbath because it is holy to you... The Israelites are to observe the Sabbath, celebrating it for the generations to come as a lasting covenant. It will be a sign between me and the Israelites forever, for in six days the Lord made the heavens and the earth, and on the seventh day He rested.' "*

In the *Catechism of the Catholic Church*, 2170 and 2171, we find the Sabbath is:

> *"... a memorial of Israel's liberation from bondage in Egypt. ... G-d entrusted the Sabbath to Israel to keep as a sign of the irrevocable covenant."*

So now, a fully Jewish Catholic, I keep both: it is a double blessing for me and my family.

Chapter 2

L'Cha Dodi: *"Come My Beloved"*

Beloved, come, the bride to meet.
The Princess Sabbath let us greet.

"Observe!" and "Remember!" as 'twere one word
From Him, the sole G-d, the mandate we have heard:
G-d, single in essence, and single in name,
Whose glories resplendent His greatness proclaim.

Beloved, come, the bride to meet.
The Princess Sabbath let us greet.

To meet the blest Sabbath, O! come let us go!
That source whence the richest of benisons flow:
Ordained from on high, ere the wide world began
Though last in creation, 'twas foremost in plan.

Beloved, come, the bride to meet.
The Princess Sabbath let us greet.

Shake the dust from thy garments, and stand forth erect!
Don thy festive apparel, my people elect!
Through the scion of Jesse, in Beit-Lechem born,
Soon my rapt soul shall wake to redemption's bright morn.

Beloved, come, the bride to meet.
The Princess Sabbath let us greet.

No longer let slumber thy senses benumb
Arise! Shine forth! For thy light has come;
Wake thee! Wake! And thy soul unto psalmody yield;
See o'er thee th'Eternal in glory revealed!

Beloved, come, the bride to meet.
The Princess Sabbath let us greet.

Make thy entry in peace, fairest crown of the Lord.
Hark! We greet thy approach in one joyous accord;
In the midst of G-d's people, faithful and true,
Enter, hither, sweet Sabbath, thou bride that we woo!

Beloved, come, the Bride to meet.
The Sabbath Queen let us greet.

Traditional Sabbath Hymn

The home is made ready. The father comes home from work. All the family is gathered together dressed in their finest clothes, and *Shabbat* is ushered in with a song:

"L'Cha Dodi,", **לכה דודי** *"Come, Beloved.*
Let us meet our Bride, the Sabbath."

There are as many melodies to these verses as there are different Jewish cultures. I've heard *L'Cha Dodi* sung to the Middle Eastern strains of a Yemenite bazooki; the *"Fiddler on the Roof"* sound of the Ashkenazi Eastern European violin and clarinet; Spanish Sephardic chant carried over from the Middle Ages; modern Israeli Hebrew and modern American Hebrew and English renditions. The tunes and the rhythms vary, but the words of the song remain unchanged. The Sabbath itself is likened to a bride, a special princess, Beloved of the soul. It is a time of great celebration and rejoicing, for in observing the Sabbath, we enter into full covenantal relationship with G-d. And in this longing – as a groom longs for his bride – there is also a longing for the promised Messiah or deliverer of the Jewish people as can be seen in the third verse of the song. As the Sabbath opens, we rise to sing *L'Cha Dodi,* and at the last verse, everyone turns toward the front door in expectation of the personification of the Sabbath, the Bride, and her glorious entrance. Thus the mood is set.

Throughout the Jewish liturgy for the Sabbath, prayers are recited and songs are sung which contain the verse, "Thou hast sanctified the seventh day." In Hebrew, the word *sanctified* is *kiddushin*, **קידושין**, which is the same word for marriage. The importance of the marital relationship and the imagery of bride and bridegroom are not to be missed in the Scriptures. The understanding of this imagery, when tied together with an understanding of the Sabbath, leads us seamlessly from the Old Testament to the New Testament and a fullness of understanding of our eternal union with G-d for all time in the hereafter. Genesis, a book of first things, opens with the creation of the world, the creation of the Sabbath, and the creation and marriage of the first man and woman.

> *"... a man is to leave his father and mother and cleave unto his wife, and the two shall be one flesh. They were both na-ked, the man and his wife, and they were not ashamed."*
>   *(Gen. 2:24)*

Sin had not yet entered the world. The two had fellowship with G-d and needed no clothes, for they were covered in the perfect holiness and glory of G-d Himself. G-d was present in the garden, *Gan Eden*, גן עדן, with Adam and Eve. Theirs should have been a three-fold cord, not easily broken, with G-d at the center. Eve completed Adam physically as a helpmeet, and emotionally as a soulmate; yet, hidden within man is still a spiritual vacuum which can only be filled with G-d. When we unite with Him and enter into His rest, we also share in His glory. Isaiah 11:10 states, *"His rest is glorious."* The Jewish *chuppah*, or *wedding canopy* used during the marriage ceremony, is symbolic of this covering. It represents G-d's provision and glory. During our Sabbath observance, we are embraced by G-d under a *chuppah* of holiness and peace.

Wedding imagery is found throughout the Bible. It is interesting to note that several of our great patriarchs meet their brides at wells, places of watering and of rest. In Genesis 24:3-54, Abraham's servant is sent to find a bride for Isaac. In the desert, he first encounters Rebekah, who offers him water at a well. This is the sign that she will be the wife for Isaac. It is at this same watering hole that Isaac and Rebecca's son, Jacob, finds his bride, Rachel (Genesis 29:1-30). In Exodus chapter 2, Moses flees from

Egypt for killing an Egyptian. Through his desert march, he hungers and thirsts for his true identity: who he is as a part of G-d's people and plan. Exhausted, he sits down to rest at a well in Midian. It is here that Moses rescues the seven daughters of Jethro, the Midianite priest, from attack by rogue shepherds wishing to abduct the girls and their flock. Jethro, in a type of Messianic foreshadowing, takes Moses in, feeds him (a foreshadowing of Communion), adopts him as his own son, and gives Moses his daughter, Tzipporah, as a bride (a foreshadowing of G-d's giving His people the Sabbath; the Holy Mother, Mary, who will give birth to the Savior of all mankind; and the marriage of *Yeshua* to His bride, the body of believers in Him).

In a desert region, water is of primary importance, a most valuable commodity. Water sustains all life. It is at the well that longing thirst is quenched. It is here that communities can be built, and rest can be achieved. It is no mere coincidence that *Yeshua*, in the New Testament Gospel of John, encounters a woman at Jacob's well. *Yeshua* recognizes her true thirst and fulfills a deeper, spiritual longing. He reveals to her that she has had five husbands, none of whom has satisfied her. Her real desire is to be united with G-d. *Yeshua* explains to this woman,

"Whoever drinks from the water I will give will become a spring of water inside, welling up to eternal life" (John 4:5-25).

After this encounter, the woman's life is forever changed; through her encounter with *Yeshua*, she becomes a bride in spirit to the Eternal, blessed be His name forever!

The rabbis of old, the great sages, explained the Sabbath as a bride, not as a mere metaphor, but to illustrate the relationship between G-d and man in the keeping of this holy day. It illustrates for us the otherwise unfathomable love G-d has for mankind. We celebrate this love – a marriage of bride and bridegroom – of a people and their G-d. Rabbi Avudraham (1260-1350, Spain) likens the liturgy of *Shabbat* to a marriage that unites G-d's people, Israel, to Him as a mate. So, too, Rabbi Shimeon ben Yohai, a great scholar who lived at the time of the Roman rule of Israel and the destruction of the Temple, wittily wrote that all the days G-d created had a mate save number seven. It was left alone. G-d, in His great love answered, "You shall be called *Shabbat*. And the whole community of Israel will be your mate."

> *For Zion's sake I will not hold back my peace and for the sake of Jerusalem, I will not rest until her just one comes forth as brightness, and her savior be lighted as a lamp. And the gentiles shall see thy just one, and all the kings thy glorious one. Thou shalt be called by a new name which the mouth of the Lord shall name. And thou shall be a crown of glory in the hand of the Lord, and a royal diadem in the hand of thy G-d. For as a young man shall marry a virgin, so shall thy sons marry Thee. And as a bridegroom shall rejoice over his bride, so shall G-d rejoice over thee.* (Isaiah 62:1-5)

The imagery of the marital bond is used as the outward, earthly expression of G-d's love for His people. There are at least ten instances in Scripture where G-d refers to either Israel or the Church as His bride. In the Old Testament, Hosea prophesies that G-d will betroth Israel in faithfulness, and she will acknowledge Him. New wine will be poured out. This is both the wine of joy and the wine of the New Covenant that will become for us the blood of Messiah to deliver mankind from the bondage of sin. The importance of wine both in the *Shabbat* service and in marriage will be addressed in a later chapter. Hosea goes on to say in verse 19 of chapter 2,

"I will betroth you to me forever; I will betroth you in righteousness and in justice, in love and compassion."

Shir Hashirim, **שיר השירים**, the *Song of Songs*, is one of my favorite books of the Bible because of its passion and poetry. On first reading, it is the love-song between the Ethiopian Queen of Sheba and King Solomon. However, it goes much deeper in meaning. It is actually the love-song between Israel, the bride, and G-d, the beloved. Judaism, which is a Messianic religion by nature, is always filled with deep longing for a Deliverer, a Savior, and *Song of Songs* is this cry for the coming of the Anointed One. I love the heartfelt cry, *"Rise up my beloved, my fair one, and come away."* To be swept off my feet into intimate communion by and with the King!!

Not only does G-d rejoice over His beloved people as a Father, but He also rejoices over the beloved Messiah who gives Himself in "marriage" to this people. He is the Just One, and He will redeem Israel (and all His followers) who rest in Him, and at the end of the story, save them and take His bride to live with Him forever in His kingdom. These are the truths upon which fairy-tales have been based. But it was *Yeshua*, Himself, who first made allusion to His followers as bridesmaids or a bride waiting for the bridegroom (*Yeshua*) to return for them to take them to the wedding banquet.

Then the kingdom of heaven will be like ten virgins who took their lamps and went forth to meet the bridegroom. Five of them were foolish and five wise. But the five foolish, when they took their lamps, took no oil with them, while the wise did take oil in their vessels with the lamps. Then as the bridegroom was long in coming, they all became drowsy and slept. And at midnight a cry arose, "Behold the bridegroom is coming, go forth to meet him!" Then all those virgins arose and trimmed their lamps. And the foolish said to the wise, "Give us some of your oil, for our lamps are going out." The wise answered, saying, "Lest there may not be enough for us and for you, go rather to those who sell it, and buy some for yourselves." Now while they were gone to buy it, the bridegroom came; and those who were ready went in with him to the marriage feast, and the door was shut (Matthew 25:1-10).

The apostle Paul expounds on this relational mystery in his letter to the Ephesians (5:29-32). In discussing the husband/wife relationship, he emphatically quotes the Genesis 2:24 Scripture where the two become one flesh. Then, St. Paul takes this much further with a new revelation to us. He explains that those who believe in Christ are actually the Bride, with Christ as the Bridegroom. And "this is the great mystery." *The Catechism of the Catholic Church,* article 1602 confirms this:

> *"Sacred Scripture begins and ends with the creation of male and female in the image and likeness of G-d and concludes with the vision of the wedding feast of the Lamb. Scripture speaks throughout of marriage and its mystery, its institution, and the meaning G-d has given it, its origin and its end, its various realizations throughout the history of salvation."*

A few weeks ago, Jewish friends of mine were married. I was unable to attend their wedding, but they videotaped every part, so I could watch the whole occasion unfold over the internet. Before the beginning of the actual ceremony, "Mona," the bride, was sitting with her female family members and attendants in a room patiently waiting for "Jonathan," the groom, and his *male attendants*, the *mere'im*, מרים, to come. Being a woman, who in Orthodox tradition is kept segregated from the men, I had never seen the *Bedeken* ceremony, which is when the groom and his male attendants and family go forth from a separate room to meet the bride. The groom himself will drape the wedding veil over the bride as an assurance that she is the intended woman, a tradition from the days when Jacob was tricked into marrying Leah instead of Rachel. In the video, "Jonathan" was in another room with the rabbi, his friends, and male family members, laughing and singing. The men were joyous in prayer and song. And they were savoring every moment of the imminent marriage, so much so, that they made a big circle and began to dance! They were all locked, arms around shoulders, dancing around in a large circle, singing Psalms of praise in Hebrew. They would move in and out of the center, and at one point formed a Rockette-style kick line! Wine was poured out, and toasts were made to the soon-to-be husband. There seemed to be no regard to the fact that the bride and her female attendants were waiting for them in another room! Already, "Jonathan's" father and the rabbi and groomsmen were congratulating him on his nuptials. After what seemed to me forever, they paraded out of the room and into the courtyard, still singing, arm in arm. Along their way to meet the bride, they would spontaneously link arms and do a do-si-do and start their circle dance again. What incredible joy! There was absolutely no concern about time, because the marriage was so close. I couldn't help but think that this is what *Yeshua* must be doing in heaven now as He awaits HIS *Bedeken*, HIS going forth to claim HIS bride!!! Eventually, the men reached the women's chamber. "Jonathan" placed the veil over his bride and the whole company processed out of the room and down the aisle to the *chuppa* where the invited guests were already assembled and the wedding would take place.

It was a glorious sight, and a privilege to witness this ceremony, because now I am able to appreciate the whole spiritual mystery of marriage in its full scope. It was as if

I had been allowed a glimpse into what is, in part, happening in Heaven. We, here on earth, sometimes seem so full of anxiety and impatient as we wait (in joyful anticipation) for the coming of our Lord, Jesus Christ.

From Genesis to Revelation, the image of the bride and the bridegroom is embedded. The last book of the New Testament, the Revelation to St. John 19:7 states,

> *"Let us be glad and rejoice and give honor to Him; for the marriage of the Lamb is come and His wife hath prepared herself. And she has been permitted to clothe herself in fine linen, shining, bright."*

When we unite ourselves to G-d and to *Yeshua HaMashiach* (the Messiah) through faith and the sacraments, we **become** the bride. And when we remember and observe the Sabbath, we enter into the celebration of the wedding. It is played out in both the Jewish celebration of this most holy day and at every Mass.

The Bible is G-d's revelation of Himself to us. His divine presence is often shrouded in mystery. In the Jewish celebration of the Sabbath, when we welcome the bride, we elevate the mundane to the heavenly realm. In entering into this beautiful time of rest, through our dress, our actions, our songs and prayers, the meals, the study of Scripture, we bring new meaning to the ordinary. We enter into a union with our true Beloved here on earth and for all time. *Shabbat* is an anticipation of the eternal union of Bride and Bridegroom: an entry into a rest when all is complete and fully realized. The Sabbath in all its glory is not complete by itself. It needs man to keep it.

Yeshua told us to cast our burdens on Him, for He cares for us (1 Peter 5:7). We are also instructed to enter into His rest (Matthew 11:28). After all, He is the Lord of the Sabbath. He is the Sabbath personified. Surely we will be blessed beyond measure when we place all our burdens aside for one day of complete rest and carelessness and celebration each week.

When we begin our *Shabbat* service at home by singing "*L'Cha Dodi*," parts of which are actually found in the *Song of Songs*, we are proclaiming the Sabbath as Bride. In the late 1500's, the famous Polish rabbi, Rabbi Samuel Eidels declared, "*Shabbat* is actually wedded to Israel and the ceremony of *Erev Shabbat* (Sabbath Eve) is like the wedding ceremony." What a wonderful union! What a joyful celebration! And who would want to miss out on such an occasion?

One of my favorite memories is of the times I spent at Jewish summer camp. Each *Shabbat*, the whole camp would dress in white – dresses, shorts, pants, tops, kerchiefs. We became like brides ourselves as we welcomed the Sabbath bride. We were a glorious cloud of white in the candlelight of the dining hall, and later, folk dancing on the archery field each Friday night, and at services in the amphitheater Saturday morning. It is an image I will cherish always.

For me, the remembrance of *Shabbat*, and then the participation in the Mass is the keeping of a divine liturgical drama that is to be fully experienced with all the senses. It is like the practice or rehearsal, which always happens a few days before the actual wedding as a way to prepare us for the things to come. So I prepare, and I keep this wonderful event in the forefront so as to never forget what G-d has in store for us.

Chapter 3
The Light of Shabbat

The Lord is my light and my salvation.
Psalm 27

In the beginning was the Word, and the Word
Was with G-d; and the Word was G-d.

He was in the Beginning With G-d.
All things were made through him, and without him,
Was made nothing that has been made.

In him was life, and the Life was the light of men.
And the light shines in the darkness;
And the darkness grasped it not.
John 1:1-5

A   As the Sabbath Bride is ushered in with song, the mother of the household is called upon to perform the one liturgical role in Judaism especially reserved for a woman. She recites the blessing over and lights the two white Sabbath candles just before the last rays of sunlight fade from the horizon. The Jewish Momma *bentsching licht*,[1] or *calling in the light* of *Shabbos*, is one of the timeless symbols of Judaism.

As a child, I always used to ask why it was the role of the woman to bring in the Sabbath by lighting the candles. And more often than not, I got the reply, "'Tradition!", as if Tevye, the milkman in *Fiddler on the Roof*, answered me himself. However, it is much more than tradition. It is even more than an honorary position for the guardian of the home and the preparer of the Sabbath. All things are done for a reason, and all that we pray and do liturgically points to fulfillment in *Jesus, Yeshua,* ישוע.

---

1 Yiddish term for the blessing of the *Shabbat* candles

Through a woman's disobedience to G-d, through Eve, the light of G-d left the world in the Garden of Eden. Sin and death entered. Millennia later, a young, Jewish virgin, Mary, said "yes" to G-d. And through her fiat, at that very moment, the *Ruach HaKodesh*, רוּחַ הַקּוֹדֶשׁ, *the Holy Spirit*, overshadows her. Divine light once again enters the world in the physical form of a baby in her womb. It is Mary, the woman, who brings back the light of salvation to mankind. (This idea would be tantamount to blasphemy in Jewish eyes, and possibly quite radical in the greater Messianic Jewish community). The *Catechism of the Catholic Church*, §494, further expounds on this with,

> *"The knot of Eve's disobedience was untied by Mary's obedience: what ... Eve bound through her disbelief, Mary loosened by her faith."*

The first words of the Gospel of John proclaim,

> *"The light shines in the darkness, and the darkness grasped it not ...this was the true light that enlightens every man who comes into the world. He was in the world, and the world was made through him, and the world knew him not. He came unto his own, but his own received him not."*

This light is *Yeshua, Jesus*, the divine Son of the Father made present to the world through the love of the Holy Spirit and the obedience of Mary. He came first to Israel as the suffering servant to bring perfect atonement for the sins of mankind, and then to all the nations. He is our light, the long-awaited Messiah.

It is an interesting parallel that in the Catholic Church, the long period of Lent, during which the Church prepares with repentance and waits with longing for the Easter season to begin, is broken with the kindling of a bonfire. The freshly made Paschal candle is lit from the bonfire by the priest. The priest dips the Paschal candle into the newly-filled pool of water. This sanctifies the water which will then be used to baptize new believers in Christ. The holy flame is carried into the dark, hushed, yet expectant church. From this one flame, each smaller candle, held by every member of the congregation, is lit. The priest chants the beautiful Latin, *"Lumen Christi, Light of Christ."* The congregation answers with the refrain, *"Deo Gratias, Thanks be to G-d,"* as the light spreads from the back throughout the entire church, bathing it in holy light. It is New Light coming to a world in darkness. On *Shabbat* morning at synagogue, we sing a song about the time when this *Or Chadash,* אור חדש, *this New Light,* will come.

As the Jewish Sabbath begins, the woman of the house closes her eyes and circles her hands above the tapers three times (could this possibly signify G-d the Father, the Son, and the Holy Spirit?), drawing the light into herself. She prays first in Hebrew, then in English:

ברוך אתה יי אלוהינו מלך העולם
אשר קדשנו במצותיו וצונו
להדליק נר של שבת.

(Baruch Atah Adonai, Elohenu melech ha-olam,
asher kiddshanu b'mitzvotav v'tzivannu
l'hadlik ner shel Shabbat.)

Blessed art Thou, O Lord, our G-d, King of the universe,
who has commanded us to kindle the Shabbat lights.

May the Lord bless us with Shabbat peace.
May the Lord bless us with Shabbat joy.
May the Lord bless us with Shabbat holiness. Amen.

Light is symbolic of the divine. *"The Lord is my light and my salvation"* is from Psalm 27, which is often recited during the Sabbath. Light symbolizes the divine presence in man. Isaiah 60 proclaims, *"Arise, shine, for your light has come."* And when we have that divine light through *Yeshua* in us, we are to be the light of the world shining before men. Light is the symbol of the divine law. *"Thy word is a lamp unto my feet and a light unto my path"* (Psalm 119:105). The light of the *Torah, the law,* and of all Scripture gives illumination or spiritual understanding into the great mysteries of G-d. Psalm 119, verse 130 states, *"The entrance of Thy words giveth light; it giveth understanding unto the simple."* Light and radiance, both physical and spiritual, come when we enter into the service of G-d through prayer and meditation, through participation in the divine drama of the Sabbath, and through the Sacraments, especially the Mass. We become enlightened: G-d's holiness shines from our very being as we remain through Him, with Him, and most importantly, in Him.

When the flame of *Shabbat* is kindled in our homes and in our hearts, it is as if the very light of G-d enters, dispelling the darkness. When G-d first separates light from darkness in chapter 1 of Genesis, it was not the light that shined forth from the sun or stars or was reflected from the moon. I believe this was the light of love that burst forth in *Yeshua* from the heart of G-d. According to the rabbis of old, this was, in Hebrew, *or ayn sof,* אור עין סוף, *a hidden light,* (literally, light with no end), concealed from man – a mystery. It will appear to G-d-fearing man in the *shekinah,* שכינה, *the glory of heaven.* As it is stated in the Revelation to St. John,

> *"The (heavenly) city has no need of the sun or the moon to shine upon it. For the glory of G-d lights it up, and the Lamb is the lamp thereof. And the nations shall walk by the light thereof."*

In the *Dogmatic Constitution on the Church* of Vatican II, *Lumen Gentium*, it is stated:

> *"It is this holy city that is seen by John as it comes down out of heaven from G-d when the world is made anew, prepared like a bride adorned for her husband"* (Apoc. 21:1).

Thus the Sabbath flame foretells not only the Messiah to come, but the entire Messianic Age as He reigns in the age to come.

From its divine inception, Judaism is a Messianic religion. Its whole nature hinges on the promise of a long-awaited Messiah who will deliver the person individually and the nation of Israel corporately. He will lead the world into a time of peace when all of creation will worship G-d in spirit and truth. For observant Jewish people, the *Shabbos* is a foretaste of heaven, the *HaOlam Haba, the world to come.* As the six days of work culminate in the celebration of *Shabbos*, so too, six millennia of our labor on earth shall culminate in the reign of *Mashiach, Messiah* (*Talmud*, Berachot 57b, Nachmanides on Genesis 1). It is interesting to note that the Hebrew calendar is now in the year 5775, which is the **approximate** time from the creation of the world. For now, a form of this light enters the home each Sabbath. Just as the Genesis account of creation begins with the command, "Let there be light," the Sabbath begins with a divine commandment to kindle the Sabbath lights.

Following the *bentsching licht, blessing of the light,* the father extends familial blessings, first over the sons – *"May you grow up to be like Manasseh and Ephraim"* – and then to the daughters – *"May you be like Rebecca, like Rachel, like Ruth, and like Esther."* Over both, he prays, *May the Lord bless you and keep you.* "*May His countenance shine over you. May He bless you always with shalom, peace.*" For the past 4000 years, since the days of the Patriarchs, it is customary for the father to bless the children. It is a way to pass on his noblest dreams and spiritual aspirations to the next generation. When I was young, not only did this blessing unite me with my ancient ancestors, but it also was a real source of strength to me. I loved being compared with these Biblical heroines. Knowing that I stood in the same lineage not only made history become more alive, but gave me Matriarchs who I felt were watching and guiding me.

After this comes my now-favorite part, the blessing of the husband over his wife. The husband recites Proverbs 31 over her: *Eshet Chayil,* אשת חיל, – *"A woman of valor who can find? For her price is far above rubies."* For me as a Hebrew Catholic, there are several connotations to this prayer. Yes, it is an act of praising the woman of the household, but in a larger, spiritual sense, it is a glorification of the Mother of the Messiah, Mary. She was, in fact, a woman who found favor with G-d. As Catholic author, George Peate, writes in his book, *Unborn Jesus, Our Hope,* Mary presented a most special gift to G-d, a gift which was

> *"all-encompassing and absolute, an utter dispossessing of all she was and all that she had to give: a pure heart, single-ness of mind, faithfulness, youthful desire and energy, femi-nine nature, fertility and virginity and all her other personal and spiritual attributes."* [2]

Truly she embodies an *Eshet Chayil,* a woman of valor.

> *"Before G-d, the spiritual greatness of a person in this life is not in fact measured so much by what G-d gives as by what G-d asks of the person ... G-d asked a lot of Mary, more than*

---

2 Peate, George; *Unborn Jesus, Our Hope*; Life Cycle Books; Niagra Falls, NY; 2006, xvii

of any other person, more even than he asked of Abraham."[3]

Today, I love to imagine Joseph, loyal and devoted spouse of Mary, at the *Shabbat* dinner table, pronouncing with full knowledge this most special blessing over his wife, the Mother of the Savior, in the very presence of little *Yeshua*, that Savior.

When a father blesses his wife with loving praise in front of the whole family, it outwardly bestows a layer of security to all the members of the household. A renewal of commitment to the marriage covenant is proclaimed each *Shabbos* eve at their dinner table. Thus, in this part of the home liturgy, the family unit, which is the foundation of society, is confirmed and sanctified by the blessings of the father. And we, G-d's family, are made holy through our faith and the keeping of our traditions; in the keeping of the Sacraments; and the faith of our collective ancestors through the millennia – and for me and my family each Friday night, in the keeping of the Sabbath. In this we are sanctified by our *heavenly Father*, in Hebrew, *Avinu Shebashamayim,* אבינו שבשמים.

3 Fr. Raniero Cantalamessa; *Mary, Mirror of the Church*; The Order of St. Benedict; Collegeville, MN; 1992

Chapter 4

Kiddush – קדוש Sanctification

Let us praise G-d with this symbol of joy, and thank Him
for the blessings of the past week, for life and strength, for
home and love and friendship, for the discipline of our trials
and temptations, for the happiness that has come to us out
of our labors. Thou hast ennobled us, O G-d, by the blessings
of work, and in love hast sanctified us by Sabbath rest and
worship as ordained by the Torah: Six days shalt thou labor
and do all thy work, but the seventh day is the Sabbath to be
hallowed unto the Lord, thy G-d.

From the blessing over the wine

After the blessing of the wife and children, and the singing of more joyous Psalms during the Friday night home
liturgy for *Shabbat*, the father elevates the silver cup of
crimson wine and sings the blessing in Hebrew. This is
the *Kiddush*, קדוש, the blessing over the wine. During the
Kiddush, when the cup is lifted, the physical is elevated to
the spiritual, and a distinction is made, at least symbolically. Although there is no change in the physical form
or substance of the wine, it is sanctified – it now has a
special holiness. The *Ruach Ha Kodesh*, or *Holy Spirit*, im-
prints a spiritual truth into every object and movement
of the *Shabbat* liturgy. *Kiddush* means "to make holy," and
it is no coincidence that the Hebrew word for marriage is
kiddushin, קדושין, *holiness* or *sanctification*.

In the Jewish tradition, both the Sabbath and weddings
are times of great joy, celebration, music, and dancing.
G-d is at the center of both, and He is the Source of all
joy, love, loyalty, and devotion. A world without *Shabbat* is a world that is completely self-absorbed. So, too, a

35

person without a mate can tend to be inward-centered. To enter into the Sabbath fully is to enter into the being of G-d. To give oneself fully in marriage is a total giving up of self for the beloved. It is to enter into the very essence of the spouse. Both are part of the reason for our creation. Our spirits long and thirst for G-d, and our beings long and search for a lifelong soulmate, a completion of ourselves. Both, when found, are reasons for great joy and celebration... it is our *bashert*, בשרת, *our destiny*. The Spanish Rabbi Avudraham of the 1300's wrote the following prayer:

> *"Grant us that we may be like Thy bride, and that Thy bride might find tranquility in Thee, as it is said, a woman finds nowhere tranquility except in her husband."*

The theme of marriage flows in a continuous stream running throughout the Old and New Testaments, from the opening chapters of Genesis to the last chapter of The Revelation to St. John. Marriage, an institution set up by G-d from the beginning, is a Sacrament, a visible sign to the world of the union between the Messiah and the Church. In Catholicism, it is united with the Paschal Mystery of Christ's death and resurrection, the river from which all the graces of heaven can flow, leading us back to the ultimate source of grace, holiness, joy – and love itself. This marriage, with G-d at the center, is the ultimate union of the Bride and Bridegroom. It is life-giving. A wedding perpetuates the promise of a future.

The late Pope John Paul II wrote in his *Theology of the Body* 98:2,

> *"We have to conclude that all the Sacraments of the New Covenant find their prototype in some way in marriage."*

And in his *Letter to Families*, page 19,

> *"The Church cannot therefore, be understood unless we keep in mind the 'great mystery' expressed in the one flesh union of marriage."*

Further expounding upon the connectedness between the Sabbath and marriage, the Pope wrote in *Dies Domini,*

> *"As certain elements of the same Jewish tradition suggest, to reach the heart of the 'Shabbat,' of G-d's rest, we need to recognize in both the Old and the New Testament the nuptial intensity which marks the relationship between G-d and his people."*

The image of bride and groom is essential to our understanding of the relationship between G-d and His people (both Israel and the Church), and between the children of G-d and the Messiah. The importance of the Sabbath and how its threads are also woven into this glorious tapestry will soon become apparent.

My family has been fortunate to live in an area of California that is close to many vineyards and wineries. Several of our friends are amateur and professional vintners, and my husband and I have been privileged to learn a bit about winemaking from them by directly participating in the harvesting and fermenting processes. The grape is one of G-d's most ingenious creations, for this small fruit is filled with sugary juice. The outside skin contains natural yeasts, which when crushed and introduced to the juice, start the natural fermentation process! Plain grape juice without fermentation is a modern-day invention, the result of pasteurization. The grape juice of the Ancients could only have been wine! The fulfillment of the purpose of the grape is wine!!! In such completion, we see the glory and creativity of our Lord. Our fulfillment is unity with G-d.

It is at the wedding at Cana that *Yeshua HaMashiach,*

Jesus the Messiah, performs his first miracle. It's a *sim-cha,* שמחה, *a joyous occasion,* and the guests have run out of wine. At the prompting of His mother (and what good Jewish boy can deny the request of his mother?), He turns washing-water in six huge amphorae into wine. And not just ordinary wine, but the best wine ever made!! The joy of the wedding is not interrupted even by the temporary distraction of winelessness. Although drunkenness is condemned repeatedly in Scripture, wine is equated with joy. No ancient celebration would be complete without it. Psalm 105:14 proclaims, *"Wine maketh glad the heart."* As *Yeshua* pours out new wine, new life (in all its creative force) and the love of G-d Himself are poured out for the new family at Cana and for the wedding guests. The life-giving aspect of the wine transformed into the blood of Christ is available for us today in Holy Communion.

> *"Worship under the law prepared for the mystery of Christ,*
> *and what was done prefigured some aspects of Christ:"*
> *(Catechism of the Catholic Church §2175; 1 Cor 10:11)*

In the synoptic gospels, Jesus, at the Last Supper, takes the cup of wine and says the traditional Jewish *bracha,* ברכה, *blessing,* over it, blessing and praising G-d for the creation of the fruit of the vine. But then He takes it much further by adding that this is the cup of His blood that would be shed for the remission of sin. It becomes the cup of the blood of the New Covenant. When we drink of this, we become wedded to Him for all eternity. It is a most holy and mystical union. No wonder the bride in *Song of Songs* rejoices in Chapter 2, verse 8, when her beloved brings her into his private wine cellar in an act of selfless love! I imagine him to say, *"All that I have is now yours!"*

To quote the *Catechism* once again,

> *"In the Latin Rite, the celebration of marriage between two Catholic faithful normally takes place during Holy Mass, because of the connection of all the Sacraments with the Paschal Mystery of Christ. In the Eucharist, the memorial of the New Covenant is realized, the New Covenant in which Christ has united himself forever to the Church, his beloved bride for whom he gave himself up (§1621)."*

Before the Second Vatican Council, the only time a layperson could receive both the body and the blood of Christ in Holy Communion was on his/her wedding day. One of my dear friends told me she so looked forward to this day, not only because of the nuptials, but because she loved Jesus so intensely and had so longed to drink from the cup of His blood. It was as deep and moving an experience for her as was the actual wedding, and it added to both the solemnity and the joy of the occasion.

At Jewish weddings, before the actual ceremony, the *ketubah*, כתובה, or *marriage contract* is read aloud. Both the bride and the bridegroom drink from the same cup of wine. The cup is symbolic of the sealing of a covenant. Both are willing partners who have entered into this union freely, of their own volition. Likewise, even though the remembering and keeping of the Sabbath is a commandment, it is up to the individual to observe it. During the Jewish wedding ceremony, seven blessings are recited over the couple. These represent in some way the blessings over creation that went forth in the days of the week. Blessings are also said over a second cup of wine, which symbolizes both joy and fruitfulness in marriage. I believe this second cup foreshadows the fruitfulness of New Believers ushered in during the Church Age as well.

During the *Shabbat* evening home liturgy at the dinner table, some of the more Orthodox and mystical Jewish men pour a little water into the cup of wine. I remember my paternal grandfather doing it. In Judaism there are two opposing natures of the Divine, two attributes which seem to be in creative tension: *chesed*, חסד, or *mercy*, and *din*, דין, or *judgment*. This pouring of water into the wine glass, they say, creates a symbolic balance or harmony between the wine, having the red of severity and judgment, and the water, which symbolizes grace and love – thus the two natures together in one vessel. In this, I see a foreshadowing of Divine Mercy in the blood and water, which gushed from the wound in Jesus' side at the crucifixion. It also directly mirrors the mixing of the two elements by the priest before the consecration during the Mass. In some Jewish traditions, the leader, after chanting the *Kiddush*, pours some wine from his cup into the cups of his wife and children, who then drink of the fruit of the vine. In our family, we pass around the shared cup, just as a congregation all partake of the Communion cup at the Mass.

As Jesus' shedding His blood for us produces spiritual fruit (remission of sin, eternal life, source of virtues and fountain of grace, to name a few), it also produces physical fruit in the increase of the body of believers. Marriage, to mirror G-d and His love for us, is also to produce both spiritual and physical fruit from its bonds of love. In the same way, observing the Sabbath as a day of rest makes us holy spiritually, but it also strengthens our bodies and minds.

A day when I can completely unwind and spend time with my family and friends, where nothing has to be washed, or cooked, or planned, or bought, is utterly refreshing. It strengthens my ties with my husband and children. A Friday evening spent around the table, then playing a game afterwards... or just relaxing in the back yard sans pressure to DO anything – followed by a

Saturday at synagogue, and Mass Sunday morning, then a family trip to the beach or a museum actually helps me to be more productive come Monday.

My twelve-year old son has learned to say *Kiddush* by hearing and observing Lou, a Holocaust survivor and dear friend whom we visit at a senior home, and from Dima and Jay, older Jewish men at the synagogue. He has also taken on their mannerisms by placing the Kiddush cup in the palm of his right hand and covering it with his left. In this way, the chalice sits in the middle of the hand with the upturned fingers surrounding the base like the petals of a budding rose. In Orthodox Judaism, the mystics place great symbolism in the Kiddush cup being elevated this way. It represents the mystical rose. Adin Steinsaltz writes in *The Thirteen Petaled Rose: A Discourse on the Essence of Jewish Existence and Belief*, that the Sabbath is *"represented by the flowering of the rose, which is the cup of redemption of the individual and of the nation and of the world as a whole."* Once again, if I might push that cracked door open further, in Catholicism, Mary is the Mystical Rose. From her, our Cup of Salvation springs forth. As my son and husband recite the blessing over the wine (they both can do the Hebrew *brachot* or blessings now), I realize how blessed I am for my home, my family, and my rich faith.

ברוך אתה יי אלוהינו, מלך הע

בורא פרי הגפן

(Baruch Atah Adonai Eloheinu, melech haolam,
borei p'ree hagafen.)

Blessed are You O Lord our G-d, King of the Universe,
who brings forth the fruit of the vine.

Chapter 5
Purification

I will bring the captivity of Judah and the captivity of Israel to return and will build them as from the beginning. And I will cleanse them from all their iniquity, whereby they have sinned against me; and I will forgive all their iniquities... And it shall be to me a name, and a joy, and a praise, and a gladness before all the nations of the earth...the voice of joy and the voice of gladness, the voice of the bride-groom and the voice of the bride, the voice of them that say: Give ye glory to the Lord of hosts: for the Lord is good; his mercy endureth forever.   *Jeremiah 33:7-11*

I've been to many weddings and have seen all kinds of brides – young girls and older women; brides from wealthy families who could afford to throw elaborate celebrations and brides who are not as well off and have simple ceremonies and receptions. There are thin brides and heavier brides; brides from all cultures and religious affiliations; even expectant brides! Yet the one thing I have never seen is an unkempt or dirty bride.

Throughout the ages, all brides have gone through elaborate cleansing rituals in preparation for the most important day of their lives. Today many young brides enjoy spa days and have their hair, nails, and makeup professionally done. Lotions and perfumes anoint the bride's body. The wedding gown, of utmost importance, is usually made of white silk or satin, sometimes embellished with pearls and crystals. Special jewelry is donned, for this is her special day. It is the day she has dreamed of for much of her life, and she is Queen. The betrothed will enter into what should be the most important relationship (apart from G-d) of her earthly existence. She will be forever united in a loving relationship to her beloved, the bridegroom. Her life as she has known it will never again be the same.

In the more observant or Orthodox Jewish tradition, there is a set *ritual bath* that is undertaken by both the bride and the groom the evening prior to the nuptials. This is the *mikveh*, מִקְוֵה. It is a full immersion of the body into flowing water. Three times (again notice the number three!) the person goes under while the prescribed prayers are recited in the presence of an officiant of the same sex. This Jewish tradition remarkably has parallels with the spirituality of the Catholic Church. The *Catechism of the Catholic Church* (1617) states:

> *"The entire Christian life bears the mark of the spousal love of Christ and the Church. Already Baptism, the entry into the people of G-d, is a nuptial mystery; it is so to speak the nuptial bath which precedes the wedding feast, the Eucharist."*

It is also customary for the Catholic faithful to confess their sins to a priest in the days just prior to nuptials. This way, the marriage can get off to a pure and holy start, free from any baggage that might ordinarily get in the way of intimacy between the newly-married couple. The *Catechism of the Catholic Church* states,

> *"Inasmuch as it is a sacrament of sanctification, the liturgical celebration of marriage... must be per se, valid, worthy, and fruitful. It is therefore appropriate for the bride and groom to prepare themselves for the celebration of their marriage by receiving the Sacrament of Penance (1622)."*

The Sabbath meal in the Jewish home corresponds to the heavenly marriage supper of the Lamb, in which the faithful in Messiah are wedded to *Yeshua*. As both the bride and groom must be clean and ritually prepared before their marriage, we, too, must be clean before G-d before entering into the next scene of the divine drama being acted out. During the Sabbath home liturgy, before the meal is eaten, each person goes to a basin with a special cup for *Netillat yadayim,* נטילת ידיים, *the washing of the hands.* A *bracha,* ברכה, or *blessing* is said during the washing (water is poured over each hand three times). Silence is to be observed until all have participated in this ritual and the prayers over the breaking of bread are recited. It is a time in the service for meditation; yet this, too, is a time of expectant joy for the feast and fellowship that soon await. The *Shabbos* is such a time of joy, that even though no words can be uttered, it is customary to hum a *Nigun* (the *dai, dai, dai* or *lai, lai, lai* chant of the Jewish people) until all are finished washing.

ברוך אתה יי אלוהינו מלך העולם
אשר קדשנו במצותיו וצונו
על נטילת ידיים.

(Baruch attah Adonai, Elohenu melech haolam,
asher kiddshanu b'mitzvotav v'tsivanu
al n'tilat yadayim.)

"Blessed are You, O Lord our G-d, King of the universe,
who has sanctified us with His commandments and
ordained for us the washing of the hands."

The priests in the Old Temple period prepared and consecrated themselves for their temple duties by cleansing their hands in water. Even today in Jerusalem, there are water fountains for the washing of hands before a person can enter into the holy Western Wall area. The Jewish person washes hands before entering a synagogue or before eating (in Israel, all the restaurants have hand washing stations in the front). The family table, especially at the *Shabbat* dinner, becomes a type of "altar" and takes on a loftier spiritual meaning. This, for me, corresponds to the Liturgy of the Eucharist in the Mass. Before the priest can consecrate the bread and wine, which will become for us the Body and the Blood of Christ, he must first wash his hands. While he is doing this, he offers up this simple prayer both on his and our behalf: *"Lord, wash me of my iniquity and cleanse me of my sin."* It is the water reminiscent of our Baptism, the living water, which cleanses us of the stain of Original Sin as we enter into a sacred, covenantal relationship. It is also done in remembrance of the ancient days when Temple priests underwent full immersion before being able to perform their sacred duties. In Exodus 30:17-21, the priests of old were commanded to prepare and consecrate themselves to the service of G-d before beginning their duties. They cleansed their bodies, and then immediately before reaching the altar, their hands were washed. The Sabbath table is a re-creation of the altar, both by the objects on it and by the liturgy itself.

The bride must be pure in spirit as well as body before joining in the marriage supper with the Bridegroom. What is done in the Jewish tradition points directly to *Yeshua HaMashiach, Jesus the Messiah*. It is a type of dress rehearsal that will lead us ultimately towards our eternal union with Him in heaven. Rabbi Hayim of Krasne used to say that *Shabbos* contains more than a morsel of eternity. For him, the Sabbath was the *fountainhead*, in Hebrew, the *mayan*, מעיין, of eternity. It was the well from which heaven and our lives in eternity have their source.

Going to the sideboard to wash my hands three times reminds me that to be truly holy on this *Shabbat*, I need to purge myself of all my faults, my bad attitudes, my compulsions, my unforgiveness, and my criticality. This also helps to prepare me for the Sacrament of Reconciliation the next evening. The cool water splashes over my hands, and I think of the liberation of the children of Israel, my people, as they marched through the Red Sea from slavery under Pharaoh to freedom; and my more-immediate family's journey across the vast Atlantic to America for religious freedom. I think about my freedom from sin through the cleansing waters of *mikveh* and baptism. How even Jesus, although He was not in **need** of baptism, instructed his cousin, John the Baptizer, to immerse Him before He could begin his earthly ministry. When interrogated by some of the people as to the person of Jesus, John the Baptizer states in the Gospel according to St. John, chapter 3, verse 29,

> *"He that has the bride is the bridegroom; but the friend of the bridegroom who stands and hears him greatly rejoices because of the bridegroom's voice; therefore this, my joy, is fulfilled."*

Each time the water splashes over my hands, I recall the words, *"Baptize them in the name of the Father, the Son, and the Holy Spirit."* I have come full circle and joyously begin to hum the *Nigun* as I sit at table – *lai, lai, lai, lai, lai, da, da, dai, dai....*

Chapter 6
Challah חלה

In the morning there was a layer of dew around the camp. The layer of dew went up, and behold, on the surface of the desert, a fine, bare substance, as fine as frost on the ground. When the children of Israel saw it, they said one to another, "It is manna," because they did not know what it was. And Moses said unto them: "This is the bread G-d has given you to eat." Whoever gathered much did not have more, and whoever gathered little did not have less; each one according to his eating capacity they gathered. It came to pass on the sixth day that they gathered a double portion of the bread. And Moses told them; "This is that which the Lord has spoken; tomorrow is a solemn rest, a holy Sabbath unto the Lord. Bake that which ye wish to bake, and cook that which ye wish to cook; and all that remaineth leave over to keep until morning. Eat that today, for today is a Sabbath unto the Lord: today you shall not find it in the field. See that the Lord has given you the Sabbath; therefore He giveth you on the sixth day the bread of two days." So the people rested on the seventh day.   *Exodus 16:13-30*

I remember my paternal great-grandmother well. Even though I was quite young, she left a strong impression on me. We used to visit her in her apartment in the Bronx section of New York. Because Grandma Rachel was completely blind, Bubbie relied fully on her senses of hearing and touch. To this day, it amazes me that she was such a good cook. She would let me sit in the kitchen with her Friday morning to watch her make the *challot*, the two special loaves of *Shabbos* bread. The breads stood for the double portion of G-d's provision of manna on the Sabbath when the children of Israel wandered for forty years in the desert. She did everything by touch, with great skill and love. I remember her old, wrinkled hands deftly braiding the three strands of dough, a tradition she kept for decades each Friday in preparation for the glorious feast to come.

She would pinch a tiny morsel off each loaf and let me throw it into the flames of the gas oven. I never thought to ask why – it was just something that was done, a part of an ancient ritual. Much later, I found out that when preparing the bread, a small piece must be taken out, according to the law of *Torah* (Numbers 15:18-20). A special *bracha*, ברכה, or *blessing*, is to be recited. This portion is called *challah*. It used to be one of the gifts presented to the priest, the *cohen*, קוהן, descendants of Aaron, at the Temple. The priests would accept this gift for their own personal consumption. After the Temple was destroyed, the priests were no longer permitted to eat any of the offerings given to them; however, the tradition of separating out *challah* has remained, only it was burned in remembrance of the original command.

In the past several weeks, I have renewed the tradition of making *challah* with my youngest child. We like to add fat, juicy raisins as a sweet reminder of *Shabbat*, and the taste is amazing! The shiny, golden brown loaves emerge from the oven, each loaf whole, but in a beautifully braided three-fold cord. This presents me with a lovely opportunity for an object lesson for Max. Like a Messianic Jewish-Catholic St. Patrick, I show him how the three braids are similar to *Avinu*, אבינו, G-d the Father, *Yeshua*, the Son, and the *Ruach Ha Kodesh*, the Holy Spirit. The braids consist of three distinct loops, yet they form one entire bread. When cut, the parts cannot be distinguished, as they are a whole and blended slice. The *Shema* prayer that is recited three times daily states, *"Hear, O Israel! The Lord, Our G-d, the Lord is one."* The word *Echad*, אחד, in Hebrew means unique one. It is a multiplural noun like the words family or team. It is not *Yachid*, יחיד, which by changing the vowels and keeping the root in Hebrew, changes the meaning to an indivisible one (I was greatly bothered by this as a teenager searching for meaning). Yet the words *"The Lord, our G-d, the Lord"* are three distinct words – just like the *challah* – united in mission, in wholeness, and in love.

We begin to discuss other Biblical groupings of a united three as we set the table for the Sabbath meal. Holy, holy, holy is the Lord, G-d of hosts; G-d was, and is, and is to come, a reminder of who He is, what He has done for us throughout history, continues to do for us today, and plans for us to come. His attributes are omniscience, omnipotence, and omnipresence. As I now separate the small *challah* lumps of dough from their two mother loaves, I feel a certain closeness to G-d. It is a time for a very brief moment of meditation. The traditional prayer recited:

ברון אתה יי אלוהינו מלך העולם
אשר קדשנו במצוותיו וצונו להפדיש חלה.

(Baruch attah Adonai, Elohenu melech haolam, asher kiddshanu b'mitzvotav vitzivanu l'hafdeesh challah.)

"Blessed are You, O Lord, Our God, King of the universe, who makes us Holy by Your commandments, and who commands us to separate challah from dough."

Soon the aroma of fresh bread will fill the home, and *Shabbat* will be welcomed in – an oasis in time, an island of rest in the midst of a hectic week. The baked dough lumps I will soon offer back to G-d's creation, my gift to our family's small flock of chickens, in thanks for their gift of eggs to me. Bread has been a staple, providing sustenance to life in all cultures throughout the ages. The first duty a woman would perform for her household each morning would be to bake the day's bread. In those times of old, the Hebrew woman would also recite the blessing, *"Blessed art Thou, O Lord, who has enabled me to bake bread, to be able to break bread."* I find it more than interesting that the Hebrew word for *bread, lechem,* לחם, has as its root the word *l'chayim,* לחיים, *to life,* which is also the traditional toast one makes upon drinking a glass of wine. Everything is intertwined ...

Bringing us back to the Friday evening *Shabbat* liturgy in the home, the bride has been symbolically welcomed, the candles have been lit, the family sanctified, and the hands washed. After a time of joyful meditation and basking in the light of the *Shabbat* candles, the father of the household sings the blessing over the two loaves of *challah.* We remember it is G-d who provides us with food from the earth (Psalm 104:14). It is He who gives us our daily bread (Psalm 145:15). This blessing is the same prayer *Yeshua* said before each meal. It is the same prayer proclaimed when He broke the matzah at the Passover *seder* table before He broke it and consecrated it as His Body.

ברוך אתה יי אלוהינו מלך העולם, המוצי לכם מן הארץ

(Baruch Atah Adonai, Elohenu melech ha-olam, ha-motzi lechem min ha-aretz.)

"Blessed are You, O Lord, King of the universe, who brings forth bread from the earth."

Just like the candles and the wine, the challah is a special symbol of *Shabbat,* our day of rest. It was not just happenstance that *Yeshua Mashiachenu,* ישוע המושיחינו, *Jesus our Messiah,* was born in the town of *Beit-Lechem,* בית לחם. For the Hebrew translation of *Bethlehem* is *house of bread.* It was not just at that last Passover meal that *Yeshua* proclaimed Himself the bread of life. In the sixth chapter of the Gospel according to St. *Jochanon* (John), He emphatically stated three times:

> *"I am the bread of life. He that comes to me shall never hunger... I am the Bread of life. Your fore-fathers ate manna in the wilderness and are dead. This is the bread which comes down from heaven, that a man may eat thereof and not die... I am the bread of life: if any man eat of this bread, he shall live forever: and the bread that I will give is my flesh, which I will give for the life of the world."*   John 6:35-51

This bold declaration and act of unfathomable love was tantamount to blasphemy in the Jewish community. Many of His followers left at that time, but *Yeshua* neither disputed nor clarified that this was merely symbolic. This would become our sustenance: His real, physical presence after His death, resurrection, and ascension into Heaven. It is the glorious *panis angelicus fit panis hominum, bread of angels made into bread for mankind,* in the Eucharistic Gift. After *Yeshua's* death and resurrection, His apostles recognized Him in the breaking of the bread. They knew this was their Lord returned to them in a new and special way.

In his letter, *Mulieris Dignitatem*, section 26, Pope John Paul II stated that the Eucharist – bread and wine consecrated to become Christ's body and blood in the new and everlasting covenant – *"is the Sacrament of the Bridegroom and the Bride."* It is the mystical union that brings us together as one here on earth and points us to the heavenly table. Once again, the Sabbath, marriage, and Communion overlap.

When *Yeshua* broke the *matzah* (the *unleavened bread*) at the Last Supper in Luke 22, he said the same Hebrew bracha over the bread we say today, but then added, *"This is my body which shall be given for you: do this in remembrance of me."* These two words, *remember* and *do* or *observe*, were spoken in the same context, by G-d, when He gave us the Sabbath. Jewish tradition holds that these two words were uttered simultaneously by G-d, so intertwined are they. Remember and keep my commandments that you may be holy unto your G-d. Remember and keep the Sabbath. *Zachor*, זכר, remember and think about it; look forward with great anticipation and then observe it, put it into action. The Hebrew *shomer*, שומר, *to keep*, also has as its root, *to guard*. Safeguard these holy things, the Law, the Sabbath, and also the Mass with the Blessed Sacrament, the Bread of Life. Do this (safeguard it in the natural – your everyday lives – and spiritually – in your hearts!) in remembrance of *Yeshua.*

It is customary to have a little bowl or salt cellar present on the *Shabbos* table. This reminds us of the vessel of salt present on the holy altar in the ancient temple in Jerusalem. It is both a sign of covenant and of sacrifice. The table at home serves as an object lesson of the Old Temple – and the Old Covenant – and points my family to the altar in Church upon which our spiritual meal is consecrated.

We dip our individual pieces of *challah* which have been broken off the main loaf into the container of salt. As I eat the light, sweet *challah* each *Shabbat*, and as I partake of the heavenly bread on earth in each Mass, I look forward to the day when I will be feasting with Him in the presence of ALL the angels and faithful ones. Until then, it is time to enjoy the earthly feast of the *Shabbos* meal with my family.

During and after the meal, while seated at the table, it is tradition to sing Psalms and hymns of praise with great love and joy. We sing both the traditional and more contemporary tunes which make *Shabbat* a delight. This creates memories to be passed down through the generations, and a love for G-d and His times and seasons. In our *Shabbat table prayerbook* (*Siddur*), Rabbi Jack Shechter explains,

> *"The unique combination, in these songs, of love for G-d, with genial appreciation of good cheer, is the product of the Jewish genius which interweaves the secular with the sacred, and spreads over the ordinary facets of life the rainbow of the Divine. Those who sing these beautiful Hebrew words and melodies 'make the Sabbath a delight,' and implant in their own hearts and in the hearts of their children an ineradicable love for the Sabbath and for Judaism."*

Call the Sabbath a delight... Isaiah 58:1

Chapter 7
Shabbat Morning Services

Keep the Sabbath day to sanctify it.

Deuteronomy 5:12

And the Lord said, "Maintain justice and do what is right, for my salvation is close at Hand and my righteousness will soon be revealed. Blessed is the man who does this, the man who holds it fast, who keeps Shabbat without desecrating it, and keeps his hands from doing evil."

Isaiah 56: 1,2

When I was a little girl, *Shabbat* morning was a special time. We were in no real hurry to wake up, and we would eat breakfast at a more relaxed pace than during the weekday rush to get off to school. My little sister and I would get dressed in our *Shabbat* fine dresses and sit and wait, and wait, and wait for Mom to finish putting on her makeup and jewelry and change her pocketbook to match her outfit for synagogue. Daddy would wear one of his good suits with his *yarmulke* and his *tallit* or *prayer shawl*. When I was very small, sometimes Daddy would let me go early with him to the *minyan*, or Orthodox men's prayer group made up of a minimum of ten men. I was knee-high to him at best, and I remember playing with the soft, silky fringes on his *tallit*. I used to love to hear the low hum of the men as they chanted their prayers in Hebrew. They would gently sway back and forth setting up a personal rhythm to their chanting. I'd hold on to my dad's leg and sway with him (this form of prayer is called *davening* or *shuckeling*). When my mom and little sister arrived much later, I would go upstairs to be with the ladies, as it was a gender-segregated congregation. Because the women would quietly gossip in the balcony, I really preferred being downstairs with the men. Eventually, I grew too old to pray with the men and had to spend the entire service with the women. It was a bit harder to keep up with the flow of the service from there, but I would lean over the rail, pressing in as best I could so I could keep up with the order of service. Yes, the women could, at times, be a distraction to entering into true prayer of the heart, I thought.

As I grew older, and in the feminist air of the 70's, I insisted on studying Hebrew worship and Torah, and on being part of the prayer service. I convinced my parents to let me become a Bat Mitzvah, as many of my camp friends up north were doing. So, in my pre-teen years, my family transitioned from the Orthodox synagogue to the Reform temple. Although we enjoyed sitting together as a family on the same level, it was quite an adjustment. Services were very much different in the temple as opposed to the synagogue. There was an organist and a choir with choir robes – very much more "churchy." Although all the prayers were the same and were recited in the same order, the English translation was used much more extensively. The Psalms were read responsively in English between Rabbi and congregation, not chanted exclusively in Hebrew. But the high point of the service was still when the doors of the ark were opened to reveal the *Torah*, תורה, (*five books of Moses*) and *Haftorah*, הפתורה, (*writings*), scrolls dressed in velvet and crowned, literally, with silver crowns and dangling little bells. In the temple, the Torah was marched around the entire congregation as we sang the song Miriam had sung after the Red Sea crossing with the children of Israel, along with songs of thanks and praise to G-d for giving us the *Torah*. In the temple, everyone, men and women alike, would be able to kiss the *Torah* as an act of love and awe and respect as it passed by, carried in the arms of one of the men.

The scrolls would be gently unrolled, and first, a descendent of the *Cohens*, or *high priests of old*, would be called upon to make the Hebrew blessing before reading the *Torah* in its original Hebrew handwritten script. Each week the story would continue from Genesis to Deuteronomy. After a *Cohen*, various men from the congregation would be called up to chant the prayers and read chapters from the *Torah*. In the temple, the translation would follow in English. Next, a portion from the *Haftorah* would be read from the second scroll in Hebrew followed by the English interpretation. This would usually be a reading from one of the prophets or books of history. Following this, the scrolls would be carefully rolled up and dressed in their fine velvet coverings. A sterling silver breastplate would go over the handles, to shine like a priestly ephod. Lastly, two sterling silver crowns (with little bells in the shape of pomegranates!!) would be placed over the handles of the scrolls. The *Torah* and *Haftorah* would be lifted high into the air as we bowed in reverence, and then they were returned to the ark and the ark closed.

My rabbi attaches a deeper, more mystical meaning to the whole process. *Yeshua* is the Living Word, so when the ark is opened and the *Torah* comes out, it's the Lord's presence that is here among us; in a way, Emmanuel is in our midst. The reading of the Scriptures corresponds to the preaching and teaching ministry of *Yeshua* while on earth. Then He is high and lifted up for all to see and adore, after which the scrolls are put back into the ark and the door is closed, symbolizing His ascension to heaven with the promise of return. We know that the *Torah* and *Haftorah* will be taken out and will be back in our midst the following *Shabbat*, and likewise, *Yeshua* has promised a triumphant return as Messiah Son of David.

The *Torah*, the *Law*, is the *ketubah*, קְטוּבָה, or *marriage covenant* that unites G-d to the Children of Israel, the Jewish people. It is the high point of the Jewish liturgy. To be asked to chant from the *Torah* is a high honor. The chants are the same as they have been for the past 3,000 years since Moses. Each note is handwritten as little jots and tittles above and below the Hebrew consonants. Each phrase has a set chant pattern, with the *Torah* chant being different from the chant of the *Haftorah* (prophets and writings). There is no punctuation, so the person chanting the set reading must become so intimately involved, knowing the translation, understanding the nuances, so as not to make even the smallest mistake. Over the past couple of years, I have been so blessed to be one of the principle *Torah* readers in our small, Messianic congregation. It is then, holding onto the wooden scroll, like the Tree of Life, chanting the ancient melodies, the Words of G-d Himself, that I feel closest to heaven. I call upon all the angels and saints from *Moshe*, *Moses*, to David to *Yeshua*, to Paul and *Kefa*, *Peter* – to my grandfather, father, and uncles – to stand on the *bima* with me, a continuous and unbroken line.

At the Messianic Jewish synagogue, most of the congregants are Jewish believers in Yeshua. Services are conducted in the traditional way, mostly in Hebrew. We have a rabbi who leads the service, and a cantor who leads the music of worship. The *Torah* service is still the high point of the liturgy, but in addition, the *Brit Chadasha, New Covenant*, is read usually both in Hebrew and in English. To hear the Gospel reading in *Yeshua's* original language is an amazing and awesome experience that I hope to never take for granted. Now that I am a believer in *Yeshua*, the prayers have taken on an intensity they never had before. I am actually praying the exact, unchanged liturgy: the same prayers, the same words, the same language as did the Old Testament heroes, *Yeshua* Himself, the apostles, as well as a whole lineage of ancestors through the centuries.

Both the traditional Jewish synagogue and the Messianic synagogue service closely parallel the liturgy of the Mass. The praise and worship of the Hebrew service is very similar to the *Gloria*, one of the highest praises to G-d in the Catholic Mass. They both have the Old Testament readings interspersed with responsorial Psalms. After the readings from the *Torah* and *Haftorah*, the rabbi makes a *drash*, just as the priest delivers his homily. Usually this is an explanation and contemporary application of the readings just heard. One of my favorite parts in both services is the *Kadosh, Kadosh, Kadosh* when we sing with the angels around the throne of G-d: *Holy, Holy, Holy*, Lord G-d of hosts. In the synagogue, it is always traditional to rise up on your toes three times – higher and higher each time as if to place yourself in the heavenlies, right up there with the angels. I still do this, albeit a bit more reserved, when I am in Mass, as it helps me to focus and makes it more meaningful (okay, so it's a fun nod to my childhood, too). During the *Shabbat* services, we say *prayers of healing*, of *Refuah Shleimah*, for all those people who might need physical, emotional, spiritual, or relational healing. We pray for the peace of Israel, those scattered throughout the nations, and the actual land and people of Israel. This corresponds to the general intercessions which are prayed at the Mass after the Liturgy of the Word.

In synagogue, at the end of the service, we recite the *Kaddish* (the only prayer in Aramaic) in memory of those who have passed from our midst. It is a beautiful and hauntingly mournful prayer that actually has us bless and praise the name of G-d for all He is, does, and continues to do. The prayer reminds us that throughout all our joys and sufferings, He is always for us, and we should never cease to call upon Him. Concluding the Sabbath morning service, the rabbi extends his hands over the congregation and prays the Aaronic blessing over us:

> *"May the Lord bless you and keep you. May the Lord's countenance shine upon you. May the Lord fill you with His peace."*

It is customary for the head of the household to envelop his immediate family in his *tallit* during the rabbi's blessing. It is like a *giant canopy* or *chuppah* over us, as the bride and groom stand under a *chuppah* during the wedding. In the midst of the congregation, the family unit shares a sacred time together feeling the closeness of G-d and each other for just a minute. It is very powerful and very sweet.

In the Mass, the focus shifts from the Liturgy of the Word to the Liturgy of the Eucharist. Bringing the gifts of bread and wine to the altar, the priestly preparations, his washing of hands, washing away his and our sins, and the preparation of the gifts all lead up to the highest, most sacred point, the consecration of the bread and wine. The priest, who stands in the office of High Priest offering sacrifice, and of Jesus, who offered himself as both high priest and sacrifice for our sins, proclaims the words of consecration, the same words used by Jesus. When he takes the bread and gives thanks and praise (*Yeshua* would have said the traditional *bracha* in Hebrew) and says, *"This is my body which is given up for you,"* a miracle happens. The bread, which still has the physical appearance of an unleavened wafer, actually becomes the body of Christ!!! The priest elevates the chalice of wine, says the blessing (which *Yeshua* made in Hebrew), and proclaims the words of Jesus,

> *"This is the cup of my blood, the blood of the New and Everlasting Covenant which is shed for you for the forgiveness of sin."*

Although the substance in the cup keeps all the original appearance of wine, it is Jesus' blood. When we receive this Eucharist into our bodies, heaven touches earth in an incredible way, and we enter into a true communion with G-d. It's *Yeshua*, my beloved, and me – face to face in a way.

There are no words for me to describe fully the solemnity and joy together that this Sacrament brings. For many of the holy Saints who went before me, this was a time of extreme spiritual ecstasy, which I have only experienced a handful of times. It is a true marriage of body, soul, and spirit, of lover and beloved. It is a point of grace that is imparted to the partaker. For this reason, the Mass, which was built upon the foundations of Jewish worship, is more than just a completion. The apex of all that is divine intersects the mundane here on earth in a holy union. I can only begin to guess at what the heavenly banquet holds for those who are awaiting that great event.

Saint Pope John Paul II expounded upon this spiritual truth in *Dies Domini*:

> *"Sunday after Sunday the Church moves towards the final 'Lord's Day,' that Sunday which knows no end. The expectation of Christ's coming is inscribed in the very mystery of the Church and is evidenced in every Eucharistic celebration... The Lord's Day recalls with greater intensity the future*

glory of his 'return.' This makes Sunday the day on which the Church, showing forth more clearly her identity as 'Bride,' anticipates in some eschatological reality the heavenly Jerusalem. Gathering her children into the Eucharistic assembly and teaching them to wait for the 'divine Bridegroom,' she engages in a kind of 'exercise of desire', receiving a foretaste of joy of the new heavens and earth, when the holy city, the new Jerusalem, will come down from G-d, 'prepared as a bride adorned for her husband.' *(Rev.21:2)[1]*

By fully understanding the foundations of the two faiths, which are so knit together, I can wait with all my brethren "in joyful hope" for the coming of our Savior, Jesus, the Christ, the Messiah!

---

1 *Dies Domini;* Section 37; Pope John Paul II.

Chapter 8
The Sabbath Day Meal

Like an apple tree among the trees of the woods,
so is my beloved among the sons.
I sat down under his shadow, whom I desired:
and his fruit was sweet to my palate.
He has brought me to his banquet hall,
And his banner over me is love.

Song of Songs 2:3,4

In many Jewish congregations, my Messianic synagogue included, an old tradition has been recently re-
vived. It has been customary at the closing of the Sabbath
morning service for the Rabbi to say the *bracha* or *blessing* over the wine and the two loaves of *challah* (a repeti-
tion of the Friday home liturgy). Then the whole congregation shares in the partaking of the *Seudat,* or Sabbath
Day meal of *Shabbat.* Traditionally, this meal is eaten in
shared company of family and friends at one's home, or
with fellow congregants at the synagogue. It is not to be
skipped, nor is one to eat alone. It is a simple meal, usually cold fruits and salads, cheeses, eggs, or fish. Bread
must be served.

This *Seudat,* also called an *Oneg,* in Hebrew, means *joy*
or *delight.* Being a "foodie" myself, I find it quite interesting that food is mentioned even more times than faith
from Genesis to Revelation. The table is a sign of fulfillment, of G-d's love for us, and of His provision. It illustrates our utter dependence on Him, for without food
we cease to live. Intimacy and community happen at the
table. All of the major Jewish holidays as well as *Shabbat*
have a long tradition of a celebration with table liturgy,
both at home and with community. Stories and histories

are shared, and lessons are learned at the table. Family and friends are brought together.

Throughout the Old Testament, people come together to share a meal – and G-d is able to work – nourishing, blessing, healing, and protecting. In Genesis 18, Abraham prepares a meal for the angels and is blessed with the promise of a son. Joseph's brothers and entire family are reunited at a banquet he has prepared for them. The Exodus from Egypt is preceded by the Passover meal, recreated by the Jewish people each year, and ultimately by the Church as the daily Paschal meal at Mass. In the Psalms, the Lord prepares a table for us in the presence of our enemies. Queen Esther saves the entire Jewish people from certain destruction by preparing a lovely feast for King Ahashuerus and the evil Haman. In Isaiah 55, G-d extends an invitation for all who are hungry to come to the feast and to consume without price. He leads us to His banqueting table in the *Song of Songs*. But the dining imagery does not end with the Old Testament.

In the New Covenant, *Yeshua* tells us that even the repentant sinner, that returning prodigal son, is welcomed by a long-waiting father who prepares a feast for him upon his return. There are many times when *Yeshua* is present at table with real folks: His family, His followers, and "unsavory" fellows like tax collectors, Samaritans who were looked down upon, and former prostitutes. In Revelation 3, verse 20, *Yeshua* tells the apostle, John, that one *"only has to accept my teachings, and I will come and sup with him."* After His death and resurrection, He appeared to His followers many times over a period of fifty days. Each time, we see *Yeshua* sharing a meal with them. Most importantly, the meal He instituted at the Last Supper, that Eucharistic meal, was given to all of us who believe as a way of sharing in His life and His divinity here on earth.

We are all invited to the Marriage Feast. We are to be always ready like the bridesmaids in the gospel of Matthew. In the 14th chapter of the Gospel of Our Lord Jesus Christ, according to St. Luke, verses 16-24, *Yeshua* tells a parable about a king who had prepared a great banquet. He had sent out a special invitation to all the elect. After these people had turned down that invitation (for such mundane reasons!), His servants went out into the streets looking for anyone who wanted to come. Just the thought of turning down or missing this climax in human history is incredible and makes me deeply sad. But the invitation is offered, first to the Jews, and then to the nations. This parable tells of the calling – both to the Jewish people and to the nations – to come to belief, to come to the Eucharistic table on earth now, as a preparation for the Heavenly Banquet to come. The *Shabbat* meal celebrates and foreshadows this meal which we eventually will all share together with Messiah in the presence of G-d *our Father and King, Avinu Malkenu.*

The *Seudat* was common in first century Judaism. When Sabbath services at the local synagogues were over, people congregated in private homes for the breaking of bread, a shared meal. At that time, there were several different Jewish sects worshipping at the temple, including the new groups of Jewish believers in the recently martyred *Yeshua.* When these Jewish believers in *Yeshua* first gathered together after services at the Sabbath day meal, they also celebrated the Lord's Supper or the consecration of the bread as the Body of Christ, and the wine as His Blood. This was done in the home of the host family and served as a time of solidarity, prayer, and fellowship among believers. During this "meal," *Yeshua* was truly present at table: body, blood, soul, and divinity. Later in history, this community of believers, scattered throughout Judaea, and later Rome, Greece, Turkey, and outlying areas, grew to include Gentile believers. For the sake of unity, as well as to distinguish the Jewish traditions from this new service, the Christian community began to celebrate the Liturgy of the Eucharist, in fact, the entire Mass, on Sunday. This was the Lord's Day, a celebration of His Resurrection from the Dead. The papal encyclical, *Dies Domini*, explains this history:

> *"Some communities observed the Sabbath while also celebrating Sunday. Soon, however, the two days began to be distinguished ever more clearly, in reaction chiefly to the insistence of those Christians whose origins in Judaism made them inclined to maintain the obligation of the old Law.... The distinction of Sunday from the Jewish Sabbath grew ever stronger in the Mind of the Church, even though there have been times in history when, because the obligation of Sunday rest was so emphasized, the Lord's Day tended to become more like the Sabbath. Moreover, there have always been groups within Christianity which observe both the Sabbath and Sunday as two 'brother days.'" (23)*

This celebration on *Yom Rishon*, יום ראשׁון, *Day One* in Hebrew, also stems from the day G-d created light. And *Yeshua* was the Light. From the earliest records, the *Didache*, written somewhere around 70 A.D., we find the first Order of the Mass and the first Eucharistic prayers which are still said today! St. Justin in 1 Apologia 67, wrote,

> *"We all gather together on the first day (after the Jewish Sabbath) when G-d, separating matter from darkness, made the world, and on this same day, Jesus Christ, our Savior, rose from the dead."*

I have heard many alternative explanations of the reason the Catholics separated themselves from the original body of Jewish believers in the first century and began to hold their services on Sunday. However, the teachings of the Magisterium of the Catholic Church, which preserves and perpetuates Church history and doctrine as found in the *Catechism of the Catholic Church*, explains it beautifully:

> *"Jesus rose from the dead 'on the first day of the week.' Because it is the 'first day,' the day of Christ's resurrection recalls the first creation. Because it is the 'eighth day' following the sabbath, it symbolizes the new creation ushered in by Christ's resurrection (CCC 2174)."*

Concerning the eighth day, the Catechism states,

> *"But for us a new day has dawned: the day of Christ's resurrection. The seventh day completes the first creation. The eighth day begins a new creation. Thus, the work of creation culminates in the greater work of redemption. The first creation finds its meaning and its summit in the New Creation in Christ, the splendor of which surpasses that of the first creation (CCC 349)."*

So I now get a double blessing: a two-day celebration each week – a day of *Shabbat* rest on Saturday, followed by the Eucharistic celebration of Messiah on Sunday!

In Judaism, the Sabbath is the bride. The celebration of it is like the wedding, and the *Seudat* is the wedding banquet. The *Catechism of the Catholic Church*, 1612, states:

> *"The nuptial covenant between G-d and His people Israel had prepared the way of the new and everlasting covenant in which the Son of G-d, by becoming incarnate and giving His life, has united to Himself in a certain way all mankind saved by Him, thus preparing for the wedding feast of the Lamb."*

It is at the Jewish wedding feast that the bride is actually adopted into the family of the groom. Through faith in *Yeshua* and through our participation in the Sacraments, we, too, enter into the fullness of this adoption, so that we, too, may confidently call out, *"Abba, Father!"* Today, the *Oneg* or *Seudat, The Shabbat Day Meal,* is not only a time for lunch or refreshment between the *Shabbat* liturgy and the *Beit Midrash* or Bible study. It is also a holy and happy time when members of the community can come together in fellowship – to talk, to sing, to dance, and for the kids, to play before they go off to Hebrew school. It is a communal time. Several of the members of our Messianic synagogue drive in on Friday from over one hundred miles away, so we aren't able to get together over the week. This is our main opportunity to see each other and catch up on all the news. I like to think of it as a foretaste of the wedding banquet of the Bride and Bridegroom: the Church and the Lamb. It will be a time of great joy as we reconnect with family and friends we haven't seen in a very long time. What a feast that will be, probably with lots of stories, singing, dancing, praising, and celebrating – with *Yeshua* in all His glory at the head of the table!

Chapter 9
Beit Midrash – The House of Study

And these words which I command thee this day, shall be in thy heart. And thou shall teach them to thy children, and thou shalt meditate upon them sitting in thy house, and walking on thy journey, when thou liest down, and when thou risest up and thou shalt bind them as a sign upon thy hand, and they shall be as frontals between thine eyes. And thou shalt write them upon the doorposts of thy house and upon thy gates.   *Deuteronomy 6:6-9*

The synagogue is not just a place of worship and liturgy. It is not just a place for people to come together socially. It is also a *Beit Midrash*, a *house of study.* From the time when the *Torah* was given to the children of Israel to present times, there have been discussions, debates, and commentaries on its interpretation. When I was young, I remember my dad and uncles discussing (with lots of humor added) the moral and ethical implications of Scripture. They heatedly debated about its application in the modern world as well as the philosophy behind certain passages. I loved listening to my Uncle Sam's interpretations. By day, he was a doctor in a nearby small, southern town. Come *Shabbat* and holidays, he was the lay rabbi of their synagogue. As a youth, he and Uncle Dave were child actors in the Yiddish theater of New York. He was learned in both the *Torah* and the ways of the world, and was not only my godfather, but my hero. To sit with the men and hang on their every word instilled in me a love of learning. Through them, I was taught to learn by asking questions and studying the works of those far wiser than I. We study the Scripture to know G-d more intimately and to know how to conduct ourselves before Him and with others in this world.

Both in Judaism and in Catholicism, Scripture is read through in a cyclical manner in our houses of worship. Each day's service has a specifically set part of the Bible that is proclaimed. Once we reach the end of the cycle, we begin again – over and over, year after year. We hear, we meditate upon, we study the same Word. We are to keep it before us always, a lamp unto our feet, a light to our path – to guide us, to help us, to give us strength and wisdom.

When I was younger, I used to think hearing the exact same passages year after year would lead to boredom. After all, after listening to it for the eighth time I'd know it all by heart, right? However, as I've matured, I am beginning to learn that there is always **something** new to be found. Whether it's a new angle or perspective – a new way of looking at the story with a different attitude or hermeneutics perhaps, there is **always** more to discover. G-d's Word is truly a living Word. It is always the same, yet always different and fresh. Before I study, I ask the *Ruach HaKodesh, the Holy Spirit,* to fill me with His truth and understanding. As I delve in, I see new things, which usually leads to a deeper understanding and clarity of what was, and is, and is to come.

Community coming together to share their faith is not a new thing. It strengthens the individual and binds the group together. We gain insights from each other. We share the victories G-d has given us and mourn the tragedies. We know we are not alone on the journey. For the past nineteen years, my husband and I have been part of the same small couples' Bible study and faith sharing group at our local Catholic parish. The members of this group have become part of our extended family. We've shared celebrations, births, loss of jobs, loss of life, weddings, and graduations. The older couples, many of whom have been married for over 50 years, are role models for my husband and me. On the surface, we come together every Tuesday night to study Scripture, but on a deeper level, it has become so much more. We pray for and are there for each other. We learn from each other. And we love... in Christ.

At the Messianic community, we have small groups meeting together to study the Bible, the liturgy, commentaries on the Scripture, and its application in our personal lives. This is the *Beit Midrash* following the *Seudat*, the shared meal. Being a Messianic Jew is not always an easy thing, because there is little to no acceptance from the traditional Jewish Community, and the majority of the Christian communities believe the Jewish person should assimilate entirely into his or her own Church community. We, in studying the Scriptures, realize that Jesus and His disciples – in fact, the entire early Hebrew Christian community – were *Torah* observant. They followed the laws of *Torah* in addition to the teachings of *Yeshua*. It was part of their identity: it was who they were as Jews. Jesus came to fulfill, not to abolish the Law. Learning how to incorporate both in my life has not always been convenient and is sometimes hard to explain to both family and friends, but it has been natural and full of unexpected blessings and graces.

Studying these beautiful truths has enhanced my life and has brought me into contact with so many different people in the Church and in the community. There are those "converts" to Jesus who think they must deny the past history and tradition, which actually sets the groundwork for this new walk. I have been meeting Jewish people who have intermarried into the Christian faith. In so many instances, neither husband nor wife wants to fully give up their upbringing or their faith, whether Christian or Jewish. There is disunity, dissatisfaction, and unrest, which later lead to tension or repression, especially when the upbringing of children is involved. Both religions insist on the upbringing of the child in the proposed faith, which can cause animosity in the spouses.

I believe it is possible for a truly Torah observant person to fit in comfortably into the Christian world. One holiday points to and intensifies the other. One provides an understanding of the other. They are NOT mutually exclusive.

The husband and wife can live a life of harmony in the home. It is joyous, celebratory, and life-giving, as G-d would have it. It is well ordered. The Jewish year flowing alongside the Church year, setting up a rhythm. Passover and the Passion and Resurrection of Christ; *Chanukah* and Christmas, festivals of light amid the darkness; Shavuot, the spring feast of first fruits and Pentecost, the First Fruits of the Holy Spirit and birthday of the Church; the Jewish *Shabbat* and the celebration of the renewal of mankind at the table of the Lord on Sunday. It all fits together beautifully.

My son, Max, goes to his *Bar Mitzvah* class to study with the kids his age. After all, he realizes that he is truly following the footsteps of the Messiah. Jesus became a *Bar Mitzvah* when he went to Jerusalem and read from the *Torah* and preached in the Temple, right? Max is learning to read from the Scriptures – both Old and New Testaments – in Hebrew. The class decides upon corporate acts of *Tikkun Olam*, or community charity (works of mercy), which they can do together. They bond. They have fun. I go off to my class.... this time, remembering the days I used to listen to the commentaries of my dad and uncles.

Chapter 10
Separation הבדלה

We build a palace in time for the Sabbath, the queen.
Abraham Joshua Heschel

Behold, G-d is my salvation; I will trust, and will not be afraid; for G-d the lord is my strength and song, and he has become my salvation. Therefore with joy shall I draw water out of the wells of salvation. Salvation belongs to the lord; your blessing be upon Your people. I will lift my cup of salvation and call upon the lord. Isaiah 12

The closing of *Shabbat* has always been bittersweet for me – and rightly so. The Hebrew word for this part of the service is *Havdalah*, הבדלה, which means *separation*. Whether the liturgy is conducted at home with family, or at the synagogue with the whole community, it is a prolonged farewell to this joyous day, and a welcoming of the week to come. The *Havdalah* rites have their origin well over 2,000 years ago. All the senses are called upon. The lighting of the special candle, the smelling of spices, the drinking of wine, and singing of yet more songs are supposed to lift and cheer the soul which is saddened by the departure of this holy, peaceful, beautiful time of rest. As three stars appear in the night sky, the *Havdalah* service begins with the chanting of a song (combining verses from Isaiah 12 and Psalm 116:13) that cries for salvation. It is a time of hope for the future and for the Messianic reign to come. Just as the Sabbath bride was hailed on her arrival on Friday night with songs of welcome and praise, so is her leave-taking now marked by prayer and music. The California sunset streaks pink and orange, purple and blue across the evening sky. It lends an atmosphere of deep spirituality and mystical beauty to the end of the Jewish Shabbat and the beginning of the Lord's Day.

Running through this part of the liturgy are the themes of death, resurrection, rebirth, and salvation. The leader, usually a rabbi or the father of the house, pronounces the blessing over a cup of wine, which has been filled to overflowing. Yes, this symbolizes our blessings and the abundance of G-d's love for us as our cup runneth over; however, as the deep crimson liquid spills over the rim onto an underplate, and pools at the base of the Kiddush cup, I see the blood of my Lord, *Yeshua*, which has been spilled out for us. Salvation, for the Jewish believer in *Yeshua*, comes from that shed blood for forgiveness of sin.

Next, a beautiful and special perforated box usually made of silver or gold and containing intensely fragrant spices (*besamim* in Hebrew) – clove, cardamom, cinnamon, pepper, myrrh – is lifted, and a blessing is said praising G-d in His goodness for creating divers kinds of spices. The coffer is passed from person to person. As I receive the spice box, I inhale deeply, as is customary, and realize that I am not just praying for a week to come that will be as fragrant and sweet as the spice inside. The odor reminds me that at the birth of my Lord, Magi from the East came with their gifts of gold, as well as frankincense and myrrh – anointing oils used for the dead. They came to the cave behind the full inn to worship the new king, but their act of adoration was also an act of prophecy of His future death. After his blood had been shed, *Yeshua's* body was taken down from the cross, and His mother and the other women mournfully washed Him. They would have anointed Him with oils using the fragrant salves of myrrh and wrapped Him, preparing His body for place-ment in yet another cave. It was a time of extreme sad-ness. Just as the Bridegroom was taken from the bride for a while, the *Shabbat* is taken from us for a short time. Thankfully, both have the promise of return.

ברוך אתה יי אלוה'נו מלך העולם, בורא מיני בשמים.

(Baruch Atah Adonai, Eloheinu melech ha-olam,
borei minei besamim.)

Blessed are You, O Lord our G-d, King of the Universe,
who creates varieties of spices.

In the darkness, a multi-wicked, braided candle is lit and passed around. This lighting of a fire is the first act of work – paralleling the first act of Creation – of the new week. Blessings are said, and we hold out our hands to feel the warmth of the flame and to see its reflection on our fingernails. (When I was little, my uncle told me this was to check to see if my fingernails were dirty. This would tell if I had done any work or not!) Actually, as you hold your hands up to the flame, a shadow is created from the fingertips of one hand to the palm of the other, setting up a distinction between darkness and light. This is so beautiful. I contemplate this first act of the New Cre-ation – after that *Shabbat* of the death of the Messiah. On that evening, ages ago, as the *Havdalah* flame was being lit, *Yeshua* rose. Remember, according to Jewish custom, the new day begins at sunset, so that could have been the exact time Yeshua came to life with complete victory over death! The light of the Messiah, just as the light from the *Havdalah* candle, should reflect both outwardly and inwardly in our lives as He is manifested to the world through our faith, prayers, and actions. We chant the prayer:

ברוך אתה יי אלוהינו מלך העולם בורא מאורי האש.

(Baruch Atah Adonai, Eloheinu melech ha-olam,
borei m'orei ha-aish.)

"Blessed are You, O Lord our G-d, King of the universe,
who creates the light of fire."

Following this, another prayer is chanted, first in Hebrew, then in English:

ברוך אתה יי אלוה'נו מלך העולם,
המבדיל בין קדש לחול, בין אור לחשך
בין ישראל לעמים, ובין יום השביעי,
לששת ימי המעשה.
ברוך אתה יי המבדיל בין קדש לחול.

(Baruch Atah Adonai, Eloheinu melech ha-olam,
hamdavil bain kodesh l'chol, bain or l'choshech,
bain Yisrael la-amim, bain yom hashvii,
l'sheshet y'mai hamaaseh.
Baruch Atah Adonai, hamda vil bain kodesh l'chol.)

"Blessed are you, O Lord our G-d, King of the universe,
who makes a distinction between holy and common,
between light and darkness, between life and death,
between Israel and the Nations,
between the Sabbath and the six working days.
Blessed are You, O Lord, who separates
holy and common."

The flame from the *Havdalah* candle is extinguished by turning it upside down and dipping it into the wine that has been spilled onto the saucer. It sputters and dies. For me, this whole ceremony represents the life, ministry, and purpose of *Yeshua*: the Light that came into the world, then His death, holding a promise to return. The extinguishing of the flame flows seamlessly into the next song, which starts out rather mournfully but becomes more joyous, almost ecstatic, with each successive verse. It is the *Eliyahu HaNavi* – the song calling out for Elijah the prophet to come and prepare the way for Messiah, Son of David, the ruling and reigning King for all ages. In the same spirit, John the Baptizer prepared the way for the Lord before he immersed Jesus in the waters of the Jordan prior to His earthly ministry. This recollection sets the tone for the last song of *Shabbat*, which calls for that figure.

> *"On the morning following the day of rest, give comfort to Your people. Send Elijah the Tishbite to those who sigh, so in despair, and grief will flee. Announce redemption for Your people. Let the coming week be one of redemption and comfort."*

I pray that the Bridegroom will come back soon and find me ready, filled with His spirit. Come, Lord Jesus! As one of the Thirteen Principles of the Jewish faith, written by the famous twelfth century rabbi, Maimonides, states, *"I will wait with all my soul for the coming of the Messiah, even though He may tarry."* Until then, I have enjoyed and been strengthened by this period of rest.

I am usually prepared to leave the *Havdalah* service and after dinner, go to church for the Sacrament of Confession. Better focused spiritually on where I am and where I want to be, I can repent of my shortcomings and make a firm resolution to learn from them in order to live a more ordered, more holy life. The past hours of the Jewish *Shabbat* enable me to have a clearer understanding of *Yeshua* and my life as one of His *talmidim*, His *followers*. The past – all the traditions – are inextricably linked in a timeless continuum, illuminated and bound together in the Messiah. Judaism, for me and for my family, is the stepping-stone to our Catholic faith, both traditions lavishing on us an ideal wedding of the treasures from both the new and the old covenants (Matthew 13:52). I really love the analogy of a birthday cake: the Old Testament Scriptures and the Jewish traditions form the most delicious layers of a cake. *Yeshua*, the New Testament writings, and the traditions of the Church are the leaven permeating and enlivening the layers which are topped with silky sweet, divinely creamy icing, binding the layers together into one supremely nourishing and artistic whole. Add the lit candles of the Holy Spirit's power, and voila! An amazing, and beautifully decorated gift of a cake. One that we don't just get to ogle over, but the best cake that has ever been made is ours for the taking! It all fits together, like the three braids of the *challah*, the braided wick of the one *Havdalah* candle, the triune nature of G-d, and the uniting of the Bride with her Bridegroom at that long-awaited Marriage Feast!

Joseph Cardinal Ratzinger, now Pope Emeritus Benedict XVI, stated that the two days, the Sabbath and the Lord's Day, are intertwined.

> *"The spiritualization of the Old Testament, which is part of the essence of the New, is at the same time an incarnation that is always new. It is not a retreat from society and not a retreat from creation, but a new and more profound way of penetrating them. As with all the major themes of theology, the issue of correctly determining the relationship between the Old and the New Testament proves to be fundamental here."*[1]

The great Jewish novelist of the last century, Sholem Aleichem, in his story, *Fiddler on the Roof*, wrote about the importance of honoring the Sabbath with joy. He was able to see its future heavenly implications.

---

1 *A New Song for the Lord*, Joseph Cardinal Ratzinger, 1995, p.72.

"What did a Kasrielevkite work for all week? To reach the Sabbath and celebrate it.

Of all festivals, the Sabbath was the mightiest, and the obligation to be happy on the Sabbath took precedence over every other earthly consideration. The dearness of the Sabbath was a faint foretaste of the sweetness of paradise."

The celebration of *Shabbat* really prepares our family for Mass on Sunday. Yes, the most ancient of all traditions points toward the concrete reality of the Messiah; and the earthly Eucharistic feast for us now yet foreshadows an even greater reality to come. For me as a Hebrew Catholic, that is what remembering and keeping the Sabbath is all about.

Afterword
Escorting the Queen

"Bath-sheba came to King Solomon to speak to him concerning Adonijah. The King rose to greet her and prostrated himself to her. He then sat upon his throne and placed a chair for the King's mother, and she sat to his right. She said, 'I have one small request that I ask of you; do not turn me away.' The King said to her, 'Ask, my mother, for I shall not turn you away.'" 1 Kings 2:19, 20[1]

For the Jewish people, Shabbat enters as a Bride, but she leaves as a Queen. In the Book of Esther, we read about the beautiful orphan girl, Hadassah, being brought up by her Uncle Mordecai, both captives in the Persian Empire. Hadassah, called Esther by her Persian name, is summoned to the royal palace, is chosen as King Ahasuerus' new wife, and she fulfills her destiny of rescuing her people from certain destruction. The book closes with Esther as the beloved Queen of the entire nation of Persia, and not just of her own people, Israel.

When we first encounter Mary of Nazareth as a young girl in the Gospel accounts, she is a bride – betrothed to Joseph. She, too, fulfills her divine purpose while on earth – in her saying "yes" to G-d; giving birth to and raising her Divine Child; pointing out the time to begin His ministry; instructing the servants to "do as He says;" giving Him to the world and watching as He becomes the ultimate sacrifice; being present at Pentecost; being present to the disciples; and being crowned Queen of Heaven and Earth after her dormition. Today, she reigns from Heaven, seat-

---

1 The Scriptural quote above was taken from The Stone Edition *Tanach* (Art Scroll Series), a project of the Messiah Heritage Foundation. Rabbi Nosson Scherman, Editor. Mesorah Publications, Ltd. Brooklyn, New York, 2008.

ed at the right hand of her Son, Yeshua. Throughout the ages, and to this day, she plays an active role in drawing ALL people to Him.

In more observant Jewish homes, even though the Sabbath concludes with *Havdalah*, there is still a longing to preserve this holy time. From Biblical times, from the time of King David, there has been the tradition of *Malava Malka, Escorting the Queen.* There is a story that David once requested of G-d the date of his death so he could be prepared. And G-d told him it would occur on the Sabbath. So at the end of every Shabbat, in thanks for being kept alive for another week, a huge feast would be prepared for all of King David's extended family and all the household, including the servants and even all the people of Jerusalem. Thus began the festive tradition of escorting out the Sabbath "Queen," which was later extended to include all Israel.

Living in the Deep South, often as a "token Jewish family," we would regularly visit our uncles and their families, also "token Jews," living in nearby Southern towns. It was a time of fellowship for us. Our three families were quite close. All through the *Shabbat* late afternoons, after cleaning up from our *Shabbat* meal, my mom and two aunts would talk together at the kitchen table; the kids would all play outside. After *Havdalah*, when it came time to leave, one of the women would always tempt us back to the table for one last "quick" meal or snack for the road; one last song; one last joke told by my hilarious uncles. As it grew later and later, I'm sure the husbands were always moderately annoyed as their wives still clung in chatter to the doorway. Uncle Sam & Aunt Sarah, or Uncle Dave & Aunt Beverly would always walk with us to our cars. We were usually sent home laden with boxes of sweets for the week. In a Jewish home, you would never let your guest just leave the house on their own, or go home empty handed! You walk them to the door, escort them to their vehicle or the bus stop, and sometimes even to their destination if it was a short walk.

Just as we show respect to our guests and express a profound sadness at their departure, it is only fitting that the *Shabbat* is held onto and escorted out with sweetness and respect. The most blessed Mary, after her life on earth was completed, was assumed into Heaven by a host of angels, amidst much pomp and circumstance and rejoicing, I'm sure. In deference to another bride, the *Shabbat*, the *Malava Malkah* celebration in a sense escorts the *Shabbat* back into Heaven for another week.

When my children were teenagers, it became a custom for us to order pizzas after *Shabbat*. Usually it was quite the little party, just because their friends were over to enjoy the weekend evening. They would eat pizza and play board games, or watch a video together, until my husband corralled any of those who wanted to go to Confession. Usually, this too, became a group affair. Afterward, the neighborhood boys would play tag in the streets until way after dark, and the girls would sit talking or go out themselves... it was a sweet ending to a very peaceful and holy day. In this way, we celebrated our own *Malava Malkah*. These are the memories and traditions I hope my children and their children will perpetuate.

Our modern world is rapidly shifting in many directions, sometimes all at once. At its hectic best, it's a place of psychological tensions and continual "plugged-inness." Attacks on the nuclear family are prevalent everywhere, from contradictory ideas to pulls on how we spend our free time. Today, there seems to be less and less opportunity for downtime or family time, and that is why it is needed even more so.

Ours is a very real, living faith. It is a faith that is meant to be remembered and observed throughout the generations as a sign to the world. In practicing our own family traditions, we place the Holy Trinity and the Holy Family in our midst. They become part of us, and we become part of Them. Our traditions, especially when celebrated as a family or a consistent social group, shape us and make us who we are. Our strength is our faith – our connection to G-d and to each other in times of joy and during hardships. Our beliefs and the way we live them out through our daily, weekly, and yearly rituals root us and ground us and point our way to the Hereafter.

Bibliography

A Fresh Approach to Jewish Christian Studies, Rabbi Asher Finkel; Service Internationale de Documentation Judeo-Chretienne. Vol. XXVIII, No.2; 1995.

A Jewish Woman's Prayer Book, Aliza Lavie, editor; 2008; Spiegel & Grau.

Apologia of Justin, Martyr; Ancient Christian Writers, The Works of the Fathers in Translation; 1948; The Newman Press.

Cantalamessa, Fr. Raniero; *Mary, Mirror of the Church: The Order of St. Benedict*; Collegeville, MN; 1992.

Catechism of the Catholic Church; April, 1985; Image, Bantam Doubleday Dell Publishing Group, Inc.

Dies Domini, Apostolic Letter to the Bishops, Clergy, and Faithful of the Catholic Church on Keeping the Lord's Day; Pope John Paul II; 5 July, 1998.

Fides et Ratio, Encyclical Letter to the Bishops of the Catholic Church on the Relationship Between Faith and Reason, Pope John Paul II; 14 September, 1998.

Gratissimam Sane, *Letter to Families*, Pope John Paul II; 2 February, 1994.

Heschel, Abraham Joshua, *The Sabbath*; 1951; Farrar, Straus and Giroux.

The Holy Bible, Douay Version; 14 September, 1948; Catholic Book Publishing Co.

The Holy Scriptures, Masoretic text; 1915, 1955; The Jewish Publication Society of America.

Lumen Gentium, Dogmatic Constitution on the Church, Pope Paul VI; 21 November, 1964.

Mulieris Dignitatem, Apostolic Letter, Pope John Paul II; 15 August, 1988.

O'Connor, Flannery, *The Complete Short Stories*; 1971; Farrar, Straus and Giroux.

Peate, George A., *Unborn Jesus Our Hope*; 2006; Life Cycle Books.

The Theology of the Body, Pope John Paul II.

Shechter, Rabbi Jack, *Shabbat Shalom: The Song and Ceremony for Sabbath Observance*; 1974; Young Adult Congregation of B'nai Israel; Pittsburgh, PA.

Steinsaltz, Adin, *The Thirteen Petalled Rose*: A Discourse on the Essence of Jewish Existence and Belief; 1980; Basic Books, Inc.

28 Blessings
40 Rest
43 Mikvah
62 food
67 100 miles
71 Parallels

20

CPSIA information can be obtained
at www.ICGtesting.com
Printed in the USA
FFOW03n0452311017
41729FF

9 780939 409099